D060217O

NCPL
DATE DUE
03 12 92

STILL MORE SCIENCE ACTIVITIES

THIS BOOK IS THE PROPERTY OF THE NATIONAL CITY PUBLIC LIBRARY CHILDREN'S ROOM

ST/84

JAN 28 1991

FROM THE SMITHSONIAN INSTITUTION

STILL MORE SCIENCE ACTIVITIES

THIS BOOK IS THE PROPERTY OF
THE NATIONAL CITY PUBLIC LIBRARY
CHILDREN'S ROOM

GALISON BOOKS
GMG PUBLISHING, NEW YORK

Copyright 1989 in all countries of the International Copyright
Union by the Smithsonian Institution. All rights reserved.

A Galison Book
Published by GMG Publishing Corp.
25 W. 43rd Street
New York, NY 10036

ISBN 0-929648-01-3

Authors: Megan Stine, Craig Gillespie, Gladys Stanbury,
Laurie Greenberg, Jamie Harms, Sharon Maves,
Larry Malone, Carol Moroz-Henry
Reviewer: Kathy Faggella

Designer: Marilyn Rose
Design Assistant: Christine Kirk
Illustrator: Simms Taback
Editor: Cheryl Solimini
Production Editor: Catherine Grandsard
Publisher: Gerald Galison

Second Printing

CONTENTS

INTRODUCTION

cience and technology touches nearly every facet of our lives today. By the 21st century, our society will demand that all its citizens possess basic competencies in the fundamentals of science and the use of technology. As science increasingly becomes the dominant subject of the work place, it is important to begin developing within children an understanding and appreciation of science early in their lives.

Learning can, and does, occur in many places and many situations. Learning occurs in school, at home, and on the trip between home and school. This book provides suggestions for interactive science activities that can be done in a variety of settings, using inexpensive and readily available materials. Whether the activities are done in a classroom or in a home, they will provide adults and children with increased opportunities to explore natural phenomenon in an engaging and exciting way. Included are experiments, activities, crafts, and games that allow you, whether teacher or parent, to learn science along with your children. The only requirements for success are the directions provided with each activity, a few common household items, a little bit of time, and some curiosity and imagination. The activities in this book are designed as curricular materials, educational guides for you to use in teaching science.

SOME SUGGESTIONS FOR TEACHERS

he activities in this book should be used as supplements to your normal classroom science curricula. Since they were originally developed for use in out-of-school situations, they may require some minor modifications to permit a larger number of children to participate. Nonetheless, you will find that these activities lend themselves well to a fun-filled science lesson for all participants.

An increasing number of school districts are exploring the use of "take-home" lessons in order to build stronger learning partnership bonds between parents and teachers, home and school. These materials have proven to be an excellent source for such "team-building" efforts. Both teachers and parents find these activities rewarding ways to provide quality learning experiences for children.

SOME SUGGESTIONS FOR PARENTS

ne of the most important jobs that you have, as a parent, is the education of your children. Every day is filled with opportunities for you to *actively* participate in your child's learning. Together you can explore the natural world and make connections between classroom lessons and real-life situations. You will learn the value of asking good questions, as well as strategies for finding answers to those questions.

FOR BOTH TEACHERS AND PARENTS

The best things you can bring to each activity are your experience, your interest, and, most importantly, your enthusiasm. These materials were designed to be both educational and enjoyable. They offer opportunities for discovery, creative thinking, and fun.

HOW TO USE THIS BOOK

The science activities in this book can be successfully implemented by any interested adult, regardless of his or her science background. Accordingly, the above have been designed so there is no one "correct" solution and no "right" way to do it. Do not be afraid to say "I don't know!"

There are twenty activities in this book; since every classroom and family is different, not all activities will be equally suitable. Take the time to browse through the book and find the ones that seem to make sense for your class or family. There is no prescribed order to these activities, nor any necessity to do all of them. Once you have selected an activity to do, take the time to read through it before you attempt to do it.

At the beginning of each activity is a list of all the materials you will need to do the project. Try to assemble all of these items before you begin. The procedures have been laid out in an easy-to-follow, step-by-step guide. If you follow these directions, you should have no difficulty doing the activity. Once you have completed the basic activity, there are also suggested variations that you can try, now or later. At the end of each activity is an "Afterwords" section. This section is for you, the adult. It is intended to provide additional information, not on how to help children but for the interest of an adult participant—take some time to read it for your own enjoyment.

ASKING QUESTIONS

Encourage your children to ask questions, even if you don't know the answers. The essence of science is asking questions, and then trying to find out the answers. Some of the answers can be discovered in books, some through observation, and some, at present, are unanswerable by anyone. Ask questions like:

(before you start)
"What do you think is going to happen when we do this experiment?"
(during the activity)
"What do you see?"
"Does this remind you of anything else you've ever seen?"
(after the activity is completed)
"What do you know about X now, that you didn't know before we started?"

"Is there anything you don't understand? How can we find out the answer?"

Encourage all kinds of answers, and all kinds of questions. Sometimes the crazy ones are the ones that work. Often there is more than one answer to a question, so be tolerant of diversity and open to multiple solutions. Use the library or an encyclopedia to help answer questions and further your understanding. Lead, or have a child lead, a discussion after the project is completed. This will help to pull together what happened, why things happened, and what the activity was all about. Just remember that it may take more than one exposure for some of the ideas introduced in these activities to "sink in." These activities are beginnings, not endings. Finally, don't be afraid to be a learner yourself—that was a large part of why these activities were developed in the first place. They are for learning, adults and children *together*.

John H. Falk, Ph.D.
President
Science Learning, Inc.

STAR TRACKING

STAR TRACKING

Be different! Look at the stars in the *daytime,* instead of at night. With these experiments, you can put on your own light show, make a delicious breakfast, and learn how to identify some constellations at the same time!

A sky full of twinkling stars is a wonderful thing to watch. But most people agree that it's hard to find the constellations in the night sky. Part of the problem is that constellations don't look anything like the names given to them. Sagittarius, for instance, is supposed to be an archer; but, as you can see on the star map, Sagittarius looks more like a tea kettle with a triangular spout. And to make it even harder, there aren't any lines drawn in the sky to point out the shape!

Once you become familiar with their patterns, though, the constellations will be easier to spot. Try picking out the patterns in these star-studded pancakes, and then go on to make your own super-star light show. By the time you finish these experiments, your star-gazing skills will be super-sharp!

EXPERIMENT No. 1— STELLAR PANCAKES

Learn to recognize Sagittarius in a blueberry pancake, and you'll have no trouble hunting down the archer in the night sky! You'll need about 60 minutes to make and eat the pancakes and talk about the stars.

YOU WILL NEED

Pancake mix, or prepare
    recipe at right
1 Cup fresh blueberries,
    or raisins
Griddle or frying pan
Stove
Map of the night sky
    (on inside back cover
    of this book)
Spatula

1 Make the pancake batter, using a box mix or the recipe below. Have ready 1 cup of washed blueberries or 1 cup of raisins. While you are making the batter, let the other people in your family look at the map of the night sky.

PANCAKE RECIPE

1 Egg
1¼ Cups milk
3 Tablespoons melted butter
1½ Cups flour
1½ Teaspoons baking powder
½ Teaspoon salt
2 Tablespoons sugar

Beat egg. Add milk and butter. Stir in flour, baking powder, salt, and sugar; mix until the batter is almost smooth.
    Yield: Makes 10 eight- to 10-inch pancakes.

2 Grease a griddle or frying pan (or use one with a non stick coating). Heat it on the stove until a drop of water skips across the surface. Now you know the pan is hot enough.

3 Pour enough batter onto the griddle to make an 8- to 10-inch pancake. Then choose one constellation from the map of the night sky. Arrange blueberries or raisins in the pancake to resemble the pattern of the stars in that constellation.

4 When bubbles appear on top of pancake, use a spatula to turn the pancake over. Cook the other side until golden brown.

5 Continue making pancakes, using a different constellation for each one, until you have one or two pancakes for each person in your family. Then serve the pancakes and put the map of the night sky in the center of the table. Each person should try to identify the constellation in his or her pancake before eating it!

EXPERIMENT No. 2— STARS ON THE CEILING

Here's another great way to practice identifying the

constellations, one at a time. In about 30 minutes, you can make your own private planetarium.

YOU WILL NEED

Empty round oatmeal box
Scissors, tape, ruler
Flashlight
Cardboard
Map of the night sky
Pencil
1 Nail
Red cellophane

1 Cut a small hole in the bottom end of an empty oatmeal box and put a flashlight through the hole, taping around the edges to hold the flashlight in place. Remove the box lid and cut a circular hole in it, leaving a ½" rim all around.

2 Use cardboard or very thick paper to cut out several disks that are the same size as the *outside* dimension of the oatmeal box lid. These disks will be

the "slides" you'll put on the oatmeal box, which is your "constellation projector."

3 Using the star map as a guide, draw one constellation on each of the cardboard disks. Make nail holes where each star in the constellation appears.

4 Now put the lid back on the oatmeal box and point the flashlight upward. Turn out the lights, and take turns projecting your constellations on the ceiling by placing your disks *on top* of the cutout lid. The flashlight will shine through the nail holes you've made, and the dots of light will form the shape of the constellation on the ceiling. You may want to make a game out of this, by saying that the first person

DISK WITH NAIL HOLES
OATMEAL BOX
FLASH-LIGHT
LID OF OATMEAL BOX WITH CUT-OUT CENTER LEAVING 1/2" ALL AROUND

AQUARIUS
LIBRA
OATMEAL BOX
MAP
SAGITTARIUS
NAIL
PENCIL
THE NIGHT SKY IN SUMMER
FLASHLIGHT
ST/85

to identify your constellation correctly takes over the oatmeal box and gets to project his or her favorite constellation next.

STAR-GAZING STRATEGY

Now that you've had some practice identifying the constellations, you're ready to go outside to gaze at the star-studded sky.

■ Sit or lie down. You'll get bored and tired if you stand.

■ Remember that the patterns you're looking for are *much* larger in the sky than they were on the pancakes or on your ceiling.

■ Cover the end of a flashlight with red cellophane, and use this to look at the star map when you're outside. Because of the cellophane, your eyes won't have to constantly adjust from a bright light to the dark of the night sky.

■ Be patient. Your eyes will adjust to the dark in 5 or 6 minutes, but your night vision will *continue* to improve. In 30 to 45 minutes, you'll be able to see even more stars than you could after only 5 minutes. The longer you watch the sky, the more stars you'll see.

AFTERWORDS

Look at the constellations at different times of the night. You'll notice that some of them seem to move across the sky, "rising" and "setting" like the sun. Actually, the Earth's rotation is responsible for this illusion. As the Earth spins, stars that were below the horizon at the beginning of the evening come into view a few hours later. However, one star — Polaris, the North Star — remains in the same spot all night, and the constellations surrounding it are always visible. That's because Polaris is directly above the North Pole. You can easily find Polaris: If you can spot the Big Dipper, the two stars along the outer edge of Big Dipper's "bowl" point to it. (See the star map.)

Another change in the night sky results from the Earth's other movement — its revolution around the sun. In summer, certain constellations that earlier this year were above the horizon only during the daylight hours are now above the horizon at night. For instance, Leo the Lion can be seen in the evening all summer; but by the end of August, Leo will have dropped out of sight. At about the

same time, Pegasus will become visible in the evening for the first time this year.

Although we don't usually think of it as a star, the nearest star to the Earth is actually the sun. If we could look at the sun from billions of miles away, it would look just like the other stars overhead. It would no longer be the brightest star in the sky, but it wouldn't be the *dimmest* one either.

After the sun, the next closest star to the Earth is named Alpha Centauri. It is 4.3 light-years away, which means that if we could travel 186,000 miles per *second* — which is the speed of light — it would *still* take us 4.3 years to get there! Even though it's nearby, Alpha Centauri isn't bright enough to be seen. The nearest star we *can* see is Sirius, located in the constellation Canis Major. Sirius is the brightest star in the sky. It becomes visible again in December.

One of the most beautiful and brightest objects in the sky, known as the "evening star," isn't really a star at all. It's Venus, the wandering planet, and you can find it in July in the west just after sunset, or in the east just before sunrise.

Other planets may also be visible to the naked eye, if you know where to look. Mars can be found in Sagittarius and Jupiter should be visible somewhere between Pisces and Aquarius. The trick to finding them is to become familiar with the constellations, so that you'll know when there's an extra "star" stuck in there where it shouldn't be. Remember that the planets look just like stars — except that Mars and Jupiter are not as bright as some stars are. Also, planets *don't twinkle*.

Although we can see between 2,000 and 3,000 individual stars, that's nothing compared with the 100,000 stars in our galaxy, the Milky Way. Most of those stars are too far away to be seen without a telescope. They all seem to blend together into a misty band, which, in July, runs through the constellations of Cassiopeia, Cygnus, and Scorpius. And this blend of stars is only *one* galaxy — one little neighborhood — among the universe of maybe 2,500 galaxies or more.

TURF
TICKERS

TURF TICKERS

"A clock the time may
wrongly tell;
I, never, if the sun
shine well."

Rain or shine, it will take
several hours to build a
Turf Ticker sundial.

YOU WILL NEED

Corrugated cardboard from
a carton
Scissors
Pencil
Protractor
Ruler or yardstick
Masking tape
Compass (optional)

There is an ancient, automatic
timekeeper on your lawn
every sunny day. Learn how
to use it by building a Turf
Ticker sundial. You can make
this simple sundial with only
a few parts. The sun shines
onto the pointer or gnomon
(NO-mon) of the sundial. The
gnomon's shadow falls onto
the dial plate. The dial plate
has numbers on it (like a clock)
that tell you the time.

Sundials have been
used to tell time for centuries.
People all over the world have
designed different kinds of
sundials. Even today, no formal
garden is complete without
one. Now you can create
your own sundial, too.

1 Cut a piece of cardboard from a carton
12" × 12" or bigger —
the bigger, the better. Fold the
cardboard in half. You may
want to score the fold slightly,
so that it bends easily. Scoring
means cutting the cardboard
partway through with the
point of a scissors, so it's
easier to bend.

2 Using scissors, poke a
hole in the top center
of your dial plate about
¾" from the top edge. Make
the hole just large enough to
fit a pencil into it. This is your
gnomon hole.

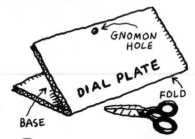

3 A protractor measures
degrees of angles and
circles like a ruler measures inches or straight lines.
Find the small hole along the
straight edge of your protractor. Lay the protractor on
top of the dial plate with the
straight edges parallel. Make
sure the protractor's hole is
right over the gnomon hole.

To label the dial plate,
make a dot every 15 degrees

all the way around the protractor. Start at 0 degrees,
then mark 30 degrees, 45
degrees, 60 degrees, and
so on. Remove the protractor.

4 Using a ruler, draw lines
from the gnomon hole
to each of the dots.
These are your hour lines.
Label each hour line, starting
at 6 A.M. on one side and
going all the way around the
semi-circle to 6 P.M. The line
that goes straight up the middle, at 90 degrees, is 12 noon.

5 Make two triangles of
cardboard to prop up
the sundial at the cor-
rect angle for your latitude.
For the sundial to work prop-
erly, the triangles must be
made according to the instructions. See the map to decide
which city is on approximately
the same latitude as your
hometown. For instance, if
you live in Seattle or Minnea-
polis, use the dimensions
shown for Bangor, Maine.

TRIANGLE INSTRUCTIONS

Make two right triangles. Right triangles are ones that have an L-shaped side, forming a 90-degree angle. The length of the sides will vary, depending on where you live. *See dimensions at right.* You will notice that when you change the length of the L sides, it changes the other angles. You can measure the angles with your protractor if you want to.

Attach the triangle wedges with tape to hold the dial plate open at the correct angle. The *bottom* of the L should be touching the bottom or base of the sundial.

The side of the right triangle that is opposite the L

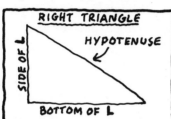

is called the *hypotenuse*. The hypotenuse should be touching the dial plate.

Triangle Dimensions

	Bottom of L	Side of L
Bangor, Maine:	5¼″	5¼″
Washington, D.C.:	4¼″	5⅜″
Miami, Florida:	2″	4¼″

6 Put the eraser end of the pencil in place in the gnomon hole. The pencil is now the gnomon. It should be set perpendicular to the dial plate. If you set the protractor flat on the dial plate, the pencil should line up with the 90-degree line.

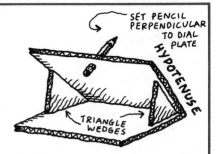

7 Find a sunny outdoor spot for your sundial. Find north with a compass and point your 12 noon line directly north. Or place the sundial so that the gnomon casts a shadow on the correct hour. Your noon line will be facing north.

ST/84

KEEPING TIME

In the spring and summer, *you* may be on daylight saving time, but the sun and your sundial *are not.* That means that your sundial will read 11 a.m. when your watch reads 12 noon. When you go back to standard time, your watch and sundial will agree again.

So make sure the hour you set your sundial with is standard time, *not* daylight saving time.

VARIATIONS

■ To weatherize your sundial, cover the parts with plastic wrap or clear contact paper.
■ Use your cardboard parts as a pattern to make a sundial out of wood. With a few layers of shellac, it will be waterproof.

AFTERWORDS

Every day, plant and animal activities repeat themselves as if they were on a schedule. Leaves fold up at night, birds sing at dawn, and we are hungry at noon. Less obvious, but equally regular, photosynthesis, cell division, and hormonal changes form daily patterns. These and the many other plant and animal activities that occur at approximately 24-hour intervals operate according to "circadian rhythms." *Circadian* comes from the Latin word *circa* meaning "about" and *dies* meaning "day."

Plants, insects, fish, birds, and humans all exhibit circadian rhythms. To find out more about the biological mechanism that causes circadian rhythms, scientists have lowered plants and animals into salt mines, shipped them to the South Pole and spun them on turntables, and orbited them in satellites. As a result of these efforts, most scientists agree that plants and animals have internal timing devices called "biological clocks." The chemical and physical nature of these clocks is not yet known.

Not every biological clock is set exactly for a 24-hour cycle. Some are as short as 21 hours and others as long as 27 hours. This difference can create problems. An insect with a 23-hour 25-minute rhythm will be five hours behind a plant with a strict 24-hour schedule in only 20 days. This may be just long enough for the insect to miss the few hours of the day when the plant's flower is open.

Fortunately, the environment helps synchronize these different rhythms. Many plants and animals respond to slight changes in the amount of daylight. For example, "long day" plants will only flower when there are many hours of daylight. Spinach will not grow in the tropics, because it needs at least 14 hours of light each day for two weeks, which never happens in the tropics. On the other hand, ragweed doesn't grow in northern Maine because it only flowers when there are less than 14½ hours of daylight. The days don't shorten that much in northern Maine until August, but then there isn't enough time for the seeds to develop before the first frost.

We, too, depend on light changes to set our biological clocks. The effects of "jet lag" are, in part, due to the different rates at which the different organs and functions of the human body adjust to new schedules. One gland may send a hormone to an organ that hasn't yet adjusted and isn't expecting any stimulus. Repeated jolts such as these may cause serious long-term effects. Similarly, a prescribed dose of medicine may cause different reactions at different times of day. A dose that will help in the morning may harm at night. The more we learn about circadian rhythms and biological clocks, the better we can understand reactions, adaptions, and evolution.

WHISTLES AND FLUTES

WHISTLES AND FLUTES

You don't have to be able to sing to make beautiful music. All you need is about 45 minutes to set up this activity, a steady hand, a slide whistle, and a lungful of air. Get ready …get set…BLOW!

YOU WILL NEED

Coping saw or small tubing cutter (see Note)
1 Length of ½" diameter copper tubing (see Note)
Ruler
Pencil
Fine sandpaper
1 Dowel, 7" long with a diameter large enough to fit snugly inside the copper tubing
Hammer
Nail
Pliers
Cloth tape or masking tape
Various empty soda bottles
Note: Inexpensive copper tubing and tubing cutter can be easily obtained from a do-it-yourself home-improvement center or from some hardware stores.

Did you ever wish you could play a slide trombone? How about trying out the next best thing: the slide whistle? Just like a trombone, a slide whistle comes complete with all the notes on the musical scale at your fingertips.

SLIDE WHISTLE

1 Cut an 8" length of copper tubing, using the coping saw. Or follow the directions on the tubing cutter and use it to cut the pipe.

2 Place a piece of fine sandpaper on the floor, rough-side up. Rub the cut ends of the copper tube back and forth over the sandpaper to sand the "burrs," or rough edges, off. This is the best way to sand, because it keeps the ends of the tube *flat*. Flat ends will produce the

best whistle and flute sounds. Use another piece of sandpaper to smooth the outside and inside edges of the tube, so that you can put your mouth up to the pipe without hurting yourself. Now try it. Can you blow *across* the top of the pipe and make a sound? Put your thumb or palm on the bottom of the pipe to *completely* close the bottom hole and try again. Practice blowing until you get a clear, strong tone.

3 Sand the ends of the wooden dowel if they are rough. Then hammer a nail partway into the end of the dowel. Use pliers to bend the nail into a hook shape. The bent nail is your handle for the slide part of the whistle.

4 Insert the dowel into the copper tube and blow, while moving the slide up and down. If you don't get a clear tone, it is because the dowel doesn't fit tightly enough. Remove the dowel and wrap it with a layer of cloth tape or masking tape. Try it again. Keep adding layers of tape until the dowel fits snugly enough to close the tube completely. At first you might not have enough tape, and then you might have too much. But keep trying until the fit is right. Can you play a scale by stopping the slide in various positions?

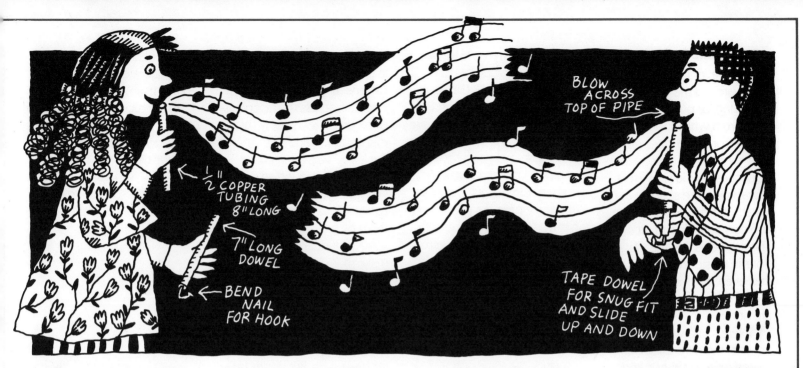

BLOW ACROSS TOP OF PIPE

½" COPPER TUBING 8" LONG

7" LONG DOWEL

BEND NAIL FOR HOOK

TAPE DOWEL FOR SNUG FIT AND SLIDE UP AND DOWN

WARM UP YOUR WHISTLE

The best warm-up for slide-whistle blowing is the always popular "soda bottle full of water" trick. Gather up four or five empty soda bottles. (Plastic ones are okay.) Add some water to the first one so that it is about ¼ full, fill the second bottle ½ full, and so on. Each bottle should have a different amount of water in it.

To blow, pull your lips in tightly against your teeth so that both lips are kind of flat. Your top lip should stick out just a tiny bit farther than your bottom lip. Hold the mouth of the bottle *firmly* against your lower lip, and blow *across* the opening—not *into* it! Try to make some of your breath hit the *far inside edge* of the bottle mouth, while most of your breath glides out across the top.

What makes the bottle with the most water give you the highest tone? Is it the water, the size of the bottle, the size of the bottle opening—or something else? For the answer, try experimenting with different-size bottles, each filled with exactly 3 inches of water. (Or, if you can't figure it out, check out the information in the Afterwords!)

FILL EACH SODA BOTTLE WITH A DIFFERENT AMOUNT OF WATER—

AFTERWORDS

If you've ever plucked a guitar and watched the strings go *boinnnng,* or put your hand on a drum while it was being played, or stood close enough to a gong to *feel* the sound hit your chest — you know that *vibrations* make sounds. But what's the difference between ordinary sounds and *music*? The answer is that the vibrations in music are very regular and even. The vibrations that create nonmusical sounds are not.

Here's one way to show yourself the difference between musical sounds and nonmusical sounds. First sing the word "hair" in any note and hold it for 10 seconds. Now try to say the word "hair" very evenly, and take 10 seconds to do it. But here's the catch: Don't let your voice go up or down. You must *speak,* not sing, the word without letting your voice change its tone at all. You'll find that it can't be done! If you really keep your speaking voice that steady and even, it turns into singing!

So the difference between talking and singing has to do with the steady, regular vibrations of your vocal cords. But what vibrates in a slide whistle or flute? Is it the metal itself? No. The sound you hear when you play your slide whistle comes from the column of air inside the tube. As your breath hits the inside edge opposite your lip, it starts the column of air vibrating.

You can test this by making two single pipes: one of plastic and one of metal or rubber hose. If they are both the same length, they will both produce the same note — although one may have a mellower sound and the other may have a shrill quality.

Modern-day flutes, of course, are just one long pipe with all the notes in the scale. To play a low note, the flute player must cover all the holes, so that the column of air is very long. To shorten the column of air, the flute player simply opens one of the holes. That lets the air "escape" sooner than it would have in the longer pipe.

Believe it or not, the flute's closest relative is the organ. In fact, an early flute called a pan-pipe is said to have inspired the invention of a water organ in the third century B.C. Organs make music when air is forced across the openings of pipes; so technically that makes them wind instruments. But if you've ever seen the size of the pipes on an organ, you'll be glad you don't have to blow into them to make them play!

All musical instruments make music using the same principles. To produce a note, something must vibrate and the shorter it is, the higher the note. A piano has short strings for high notes and long strings for low notes. But violins have only four strings and they all seem to be the same length. How do you get high notes on a violin? The musician shortens the string — or really shortens the length a string can vibrate — by holding the string tightly against the neck of the violin with his or her fingers.

If you've ever wondered how the air in a trumpet can be made shorter or longer, just look at all those twists and turns in the tubing. The valves on a trumpet open and close certain sections of tubing to change the overall length. On a slide trombone, you can *see* how the tubing is made longer. Just like on your slide whistle, the slide moves in and out to change the length of the column of air. On trumpets and trombones, something else vibrates too: the player's lips!

TIME OUT

TIME OUT

Got a minute? Great—but you'll need more than that to make the timekeepers in this timely activity. Allow about 15 minutes to set up each "clock"—and then plan to *watch* them (excuse the pun) for an hour or so!

YOU WILL NEED

An 8" piece of cotton string
Vegetable oil
Heavy-duty aluminum foil or pie pan
Matches
A watch or stopwatch
2 Identical straight-sided candles (not tapers)
Candlesticks (or Plasticine, or modeling clay, to hold candles upright)
Small nail
Empty milk carton
Ballpoint pen
5 Identical paper or Styrofoam cups
Large cardboard box
Brass paper fasteners (with a head and two prongs)
Empty jar
2 Small plastic soda bottles
Heavy-duty tape
Box of table salt

When the ref calls "Time out!"—how does he know when to call "Time in?" He uses his stopwatch, of course. These days we have lots of timekeepers—from digital watches to Big Ben, London's famous clock tower. But in ancient times, finding ways to measure time was a problem. How could a peasant bake bread if he didn't know how long to leave it in the oven? Here are some clocks, timers, and stopwatches that were used a long, long time ago. Make them all and then compare: Which clock is the most accurate? Which one would you use if you really wanted to be on time?

A String Timer

Cut a piece of cotton string 8" long. Knot the string at every inch, trying to keep the spaces between the knots equal. Pour a small amount of vegetable oil in a small dish and soak the string in the oil. Lay the oily string on an aluminum pie pan or on a piece of heavy-duty aluminum foil with the edges turned up. Place the aluminum pan in the kitchen sink for safety.

Have an adult help with the next step. Light one end of the string and let it burn on the aluminum pan. Make sure the aluminum pan is lying flat—or with the lighted end of the string slightly uphill. Otherwise the string won't burn evenly.

How long does it take for the string to burn from one knot to the next? Time it with a watch or stopwatch. How long does an 8" string burn?

A Candle Timer

Place two identical straight-sided candles in candlesticks. Or set them side by side on an aluminum pie pan and hold the candles in place with small blobs of Plasticine or modeling clay. Ask an adult's help to light one of the candles. **Be sure to keep your hair and clothing away from the flame.** Let the candle burn for exactly 10 minutes. Blow out the flame. How far has it burned? Hold the first candle next to the other one. Use a nail to scratch a ring around the other candle to show how far down it will burn in 10 minutes. Continue scratching rings, equally spaced, around the candles. Each mark represents 10 minutes. Light one of the candles again and burn three sections. Time the Candle Timer. How accurate was it? Did the three 10-minute sections burn for 30 minutes? Which clock is more accurate: the String Timer or the Candle Timer?

A Water Timer

Open up the top of an empty milk carton and rinse it. Use a ballpoint pen to mark equally spaced lines on the inside of the carton. Poke a small hole in the side of the carton, about an inch from the bottom.

Fill the carton with water and let the water run out the hole into the sink. How long does it take for the water to go down from the top line to the next line? Is the emptying time between each line the same? Or does the water empty more slowly as it drains? Is this an accurate clock?

USE A NAIL TO SCRATCH RINGS

USE A BALL POINT PEN TO MARK EQUALLY SPACED LINES ON THE INSIDE OF CARTON

POKE A HOLE IN BOTTOM OF **5** IDENTICAL STYROFOAM CUPS AND FASTEN IN A ROW ONE ABOVE EACH OTHER

SCRATCH AROUND OTHER CANDLE

CLOCK

ST/88

REYNOLDS

PASTEURIZED AND HOMOGENIZED **MILK**

SPOUT

TO OPEN

MILK

PASTEURIZED HOMOGENIZED VITAMIN D

ONE QUART

POKE A HOLE ABOUT ONE INCH FROM BOTTOM

WEIGHT INSIDE OF BOX WITH BOOKS OR ROCKS

USE BRASS PAPER FASTENER TO FASTEN CUPS TO SIDE OF BOX.

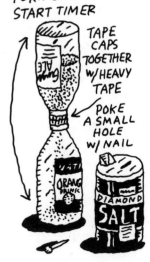

TURN OVER TO START TIMER

TAPE CAPS TOGETHER W/HEAVY TAPE

POKE A SMALL HOLE W/ NAIL

ORANG DRINK

DIAMOND SALT

A Deluxe Water Timer

Poke one hole in the bottom of each of 5 identical paper or Styrofoam cups. Fasten the cups in a row, one above the other, to the outside of a cardboard box. To fasten them, use brass paper fasteners poked through the cups and the box. Weight the inside of the box with rocks or books, so it won't tip over. Put an empty jar under the bottom cup to catch the water.

Measure out one full cup of water and pour it into the top cup. How long does it take the water to run through each cup? How long to reach the bottom? Repeat the experiment and time it carefully. Is the Deluxe Water Timer more accurate or less accurate than the other clocks you have made?

An Hourglass—or a 3-Minute Timer?

Wash and completely dry the insides of two small plastic soft-drink bottles. (The 16-ounce size works best.) Remove both caps and use heavy-duty tape to tape them together with their top sides touching. Use a nail to poke a small hole straight through both bottle caps. Fill one bottle three-fourths full of ordinary table salt. Screw on the double lid. Turn the other bottle upside down on top of the one filled with salt. Screw it to the double cap. To start your timer, simply turn it over and watch the salt run from the top bottle to the bottom. How long does it take? You might want to adjust the amount of salt in the timer so that it takes exactly 3 minutes for the salt to run out.

Which of the clocks that you made is the most reliable and accurate?

AFTERWORDS

What's the biggest clock in the world? According to the *Guinness Book of World Records,* you have your choice. The biggest clock *face*—the floral clock in Hokkaido, Japan—is more than 59 feet in diameter. The most *massive* clock is located in the Cathedral of St. Pierre in Beauvais, France. And the largest four-faced clock, with each face 40 feet in diameter, is on the building of the Allen-Bradley Co. in Milwaukee, Wisconsin.

But hold on a second … and look down. You're actually *standing on* the biggest timekeeper known to man. Earth, as it goes around the sun, is the "clock" that tells us when it's day or night, when it's summer, winter, spring, or fall. All of the other clocks and timepieces we use are designed to measure—and to put a name or a number on—the chunks of time we experience. But for centuries, people had no better way to tell time than to look up at the position of the sun in the sky. But it's not so easy to measure out smaller segments of time—like an hour—by simply

looking up. That's why people invented clocks.

Perhaps the oldest clock known is the sundial, which was invented more than 4,000 years ago. Water and candle clocks too, while not as ancient as the sundial, are very early clocks. The Greeks used water clocks called *clepsydras,* which means "thief of water," to time speeches made by lawyers during trials. Judges wanted to be sure that each lawyer was given the same amount of time to plead a case. Another timekeeper used in the courts was the hourglass full of sand. Each person was allowed to speak until the sand (time) ran out from the upper chamber into the lower chamber—thus the expression "time is running out"!

One of the biggest advances in the measurement of time started in a church in 1581. Seventeen-year-old Galileo Galilei became bored with the church service and started watching the swinging lights hanging overhead. He noticed that no matter how far the lights swung, they always seemed to take the same amount of

time to complete a swing. He used his own pulse to time the swings. Galileo figured that anything that moved in such a regular way could probably be used to measure time. Later on, pendulum clocks were invented. These clocks use a weight that falls slowly to give small pulses of energy to each swing. However, a swinging weight in a clock is of no use to a ship tossing at sea. So in 1761, John Harrison invented a wind-up clock that was accurate.

Today, we have many very accurate timekeepers—so your candle clock is rather out of date. Quartz-crystal timepieces, which were invented in the 1920s, are accurate to within $\frac{1}{1,000}$ *of a second* each 6 months. Atomic clocks, invented in the 1950s, are even more accurate. In fact, the world's *most* accurate clock is an atomic clock in the U.S. Naval Research Laboratory in Washington, D.C. It would take 1.7 *million* years for this clock to gain or lose one second! By the way, what time *is* it?

HIDDEN RAINBOWS

HIDDEN RAINBOWS

Beautiful sunsets, forest scenes, and colorful rainbows can be found hiding deep in the stroke of your pen. How do you release them for your viewing pleasure? The secret is a technique called *paper chromatography* and will take you less than an hour to discover.

YOU WILL NEED

1 Package of coffee filters
Scissors
Several rubber bands
1 Dishpan, large bowl, or other basin at least 4" deep
Tape
1 Set of colored marking pens, *water soluble*
Old newspaper
1 Set of liquid food colorings, small size
Paper plates
Toothpicks
1 Package of M&M candies
Deep-colored fruits and vegetables
Vinegar or rubbing alcohol

1 Cut a bunch of strips of filter paper about ¾" wide and 4" long. Then cut 2 or 3 rubber bands, stretch them across the basin, and tape them in place. Fold one of the paper strips over ½" at the end, and hang it on one of the rubber bands. Put just enough water into the basin to bring the water up to the end of the paper.

2 Select a pen from your set. Use it to draw a line across the width of one of the paper strips, ½" from the bottom. Fold the top of the strip over ½", and hang it on the rubber band. Watch the water wick up the paper, doing its magic on the ink mark as it moves upward.

3 Try all of the colors you can find. Blacks, browns, and dark greens are particularly interesting. Try to find a number of different brands of pens in these dark colors. When the colors have moved as far up the paper as they can (in about 5 minutes), lay them on old newspaper to dry.

VARIATIONS

■ Use your chromatography set-up to find out how food colorings move. Mix drops of food colors on a paper plate to make your own inks, and see if the original colors can be separated out. Use toothpicks to mix the drops of color and to put the marks on the paper strips.

■ Use your set of pens to make many different color marks on paper strips. See what happens when they get absorbed up the paper.

■ Use larger pieces of paper, and draw little pictures and designs on them. Hang them in the basin and watch the modern art unfold.

■ Dip an M&M candy in water, and transfer the color to a strip of paper. Discover the rainbows in the treats you sometimes eat.

■ Test the movement of natural colors, called *pigments*. Try beets, cherries, blueberries, spinach, and other heavily pigmented plants. You can transfer the pigment by putting a little sample of the material on the paper, and smashing the juice onto the paper.

■ Some pigments will not move in water, but might when other solvents are used. Try vinegar (an acid), rubbing alcohol, ammonia or paint thinner. Remember, these solvents should be used with adult supervision, and they are best used outdoors.

DRAW A LINE ACROSS THE WIDTH OF THE STRIPS

HANG FILTER STRIPS FROM RUBBER BANDS INTO BASIN OF WATER

YOU CAN TRY MANY DIFFERENT COLORS

VINEGAR

GRAPE JUICE

COFFEE FILTERS

PAINT THINNER

ST/86

AFTERWORDS

While you were having fun discovering hidden rainbows, you were actually dealing with a branch of science called *chromatography*. In Greek, *chroma* meant "color" and *graph* meant "to write." Scientists use this "color writing" to identify different substances.

In your chromatography, you used filter paper, which operates on the principle of *capillarity*. You probably already know that your blood flows through some very small veins called *capillaries*. (Capillary means "tiny tube.")

But where are the tubes in paper? Any paper is made up of tiny fibers that are pressed close together. There are spaces between these fibers that can act like tiny tubes. Suppose you had two walls of fibers and you put them very close together (closer than you can see without a microscope). A water droplet sitting between these two walls would look like this:

WATER DROPLET
FIBERS ACT LIKE WALLS
FIBER
TINY TUBE

You can see that the sides of the droplet are pulled *up* against the walls and the top of the droplet is curved *down*. Two sets of forces are at work here. *Cohesive* forces within the droplet are working between the water molecules to keep the droplet together. At the same time, *adhesive* forces in the paper fibers try to pull, or absorb, the water molecules up into the walls. It's like a tug-of-war!

As long as the adhesive forces are stronger, the water will wet the walls. This means that water will be pulled up the fiber tubes by a process called *capillary action*. When the cohesive forces between the water molecules becomes equal to the adhesive forces between the water and the fiber walls, the water stops rising up the paper.

Next, think of the last time you saw a rain spout on the side of a building. If water was pouring out onto gravel underneath, you'd find the largest pebbles directly under the spout. The lighter pebbles were picked up by the water current and carried away. As the current grows weaker, the larger rocks drop out of the stream. The lightest particles get carried the farthest away from the rain spout.

So, if you find that a green pen mark leaves a blue band of color with a yellow band above it, you now know at least two things: (1) the green pigment in the pen is actually made up of two colors, blue and yellow; and (2) the yellow color particles weigh less than the blue. Just like sand pebbles in a stream, the yellow was carried farther away, outside the blue.

Colors occur naturally in our most important organic sources (like the chemicals produced by plants and animals — especially plants). Scientists then use chromatography to separate and identify these substances by their color. From there, they can figure out how to make their own organic chemicals in the laboratory. Their chromatography is very sophisticated, but the results are no more colorful than your *own* Hidden Rainbows.

3-D VIEWER

3-D VIEWER

Take a look into the third dimension—with this fantastic 3-D Viewer! You can use your own camera to take the pictures. After the pictures are developed, you'll need about 20 minutes to make the viewer.

YOU WILL NEED

A camera
Print film for your camera
Tape measure or yardstick
Cardboard tube at least 2" in
    diameter and 24" long
    (or you can use two
    tubes, each 12" long)
Scissors
Felt-tip marker or pen
Pencil
Transparent tape

Years ago, 3-D Viewers were called *stereoscopes*. Each stereoscope held two pictures of the same scene. But each picture was taken from a slightly different point of view. Normally when you look at a photograph, you see only two dimensions: height and width—a flat image. But if you looked at one picture with one eye and the other picture with the other eye through a stereoscope, you would see an eye-popping 3-D scene—one with height, width, *and* depth. You can easily make a 3-D viewer that will transform your own photographs into amazingly lifelike scenes. But don't forget to buy extra film because there's a trick to it: You've got to photograph everything twice!

EXPERIMENT WITH YOUR EYES

Before you make your 3-D Viewer, you should find out a little bit about how you see. First, measure the distance between your eyes. If you are a grown-up (but not a *giant*!), your eyes are probably about 2½" apart, maybe a little less. Do you think each eye sees the same thing? Find out by holding up one finger in front of your face, about 6" away. Close your right eye and observe where your finger seems to be. Line your finger up with something vertical, like a doorway. Then open your right eye and close the left. Your finger will seem to "jump" back and forth, from one side of the doorway to the other. That's because you are seeing your finger differently, depending on which eye you use. Your right eye and your left eye see two different "pictures," from two different angles. When your brain puts the two pictures together, you see things three-dimensionally.

TAKING 3-D PICTURES

Please read all of the instructions below, *before* you begin photographing. That way you will be sure to get good results.

You can use any ordinary camera to take 3-D pictures. Simply load your camera and go outside on a fairly bright day. The idea is to take two pictures of the same scene, separated by about 2½", since that's the way your eyes see.

There are two good ways to take 3-D pictures. Method No. 1 is very easy. You simply hold the camera up to your right eye and take the picture. Then, for the second picture in the set, you hold the camera up to your left eye. This will automatically move the camera about 2½" to the left. If you use this method, you must hold your head very still between the two pictures, so that your angle of view doesn't change.

For Method No. 2, you put the camera on a table or another solid surface. Put a tape measure or yardstick behind the camera, parallel to it. Take your first picture, then move the camera exactly 2½" to the left. Now take the second picture. Again, you must be sure that the camera isn't twisted or turned between pictures.

HINTS FOR SUCCESS

■ Be sure to photograph every scene twice!

■ 3-D pictures work best if the different objects in the picture are at different distances from the camera. For instance, you might have a bicycle in the foreground. There could be some trees about 4' behind the bicycle. The sky would be your distant background.

■ Don't put the main subject *too* close to the camera lens. The main subject should be at least 5' away from the camera.

■ Remember that the subject and the background must remain exactly the same for both pictures. If you are photographing a street scene, be sure to take the second picture quickly— before a car moves, for instance—so that the street scene will be unchanged. If you are photographing a person, he or she must remain perfectly still for both pictures. Don't let your subject smile in Picture 1 and then frown in Picture 2!

■ The pictures you take will need to be cut so that they fit in the 3-D Viewer. Only part of each picture will be used. Remember this when you are composing your scene. Try to keep all of the important elements in the center of the "frame," or camera viewfinder.

MAKING THE 3-D VIEWER

You will need to start with a long cardboard tube, like the ones used to hold gift-wrapping paper. It should be at least 2" in diameter and at least 24" long. Cut the tube into two pieces, each 12" long. (If the tube is longer, cut off the extra length and discard it.) With a marker or pen, label one tube LEFT and the other one RIGHT.

If you don't have a cardboard tube, you can use stiff white paper. Use two sheets of paper, 8½" × 11". Roll each one into an 11" tube that is 2" in diameter.

Now hold the tubes up to your eyes and look toward a light. If the tubes are not held closely together, you will see two circles of light at the ends. But if the tubes are held tightly together at the far end, and *just slightly* separated at your eyes, the two circles of light will come together. You will be looking through two tubes, but seeing only one circle. Good! Now you know how to hold the tubes when you are viewing in 3-D.

VIEWING THE 3-D PICTURES

Remember that you photographed each scene or subject twice.

Find a set of two developed prints and look to make sure they are slightly different. You will notice that in one picture you can see a little more of the right side of the scene—or more of the right side of the *background*. That picture goes on the RIGHT tube. The other picture, showing more of the left, goes on the LEFT tube. Put both pictures, face up, together like a sandwich, and set them down on a flat surface. Stand one of the

LEFT PICTURE

RIGHT PICTURE

MARK THE TUBES LEFT AND RIGHT

YOU CAN USE YOUR CAMERA TO TAKE 3-D PICTURES

tubes up on the main part of the picture and, using a pencil, trace around the outside of the tube.

Now cut out the circle from the pictures, cutting right through both prints at once. You will then have two circular photographs, each a little bit larger than the diameter of the tubes. Tape the right picture to the RIGHT tube and the left picture to the LEFT tube, with the pictures facing in.

Hold the tubes together and face a light source. At first, you might see two images or pictures. But slowly, the two pictures will *converge* in your mind, and you will see only one—just as you saw only one circle of light. Be patient. Sometimes it takes a minute or so for your mind to bring the two pictures together. When they do come together, you will see that your main subject stands out from the background in a very three-dimensional way!

AFTERWORDS

Hold on to your seats, horror fans. Here comes a hideously disfigured man in a black cape, with a face that looks like it's been through a three-alarm fire. (It has!) He's about to thrust his gnarled hand out at you, but you're not frightened, are you? After all—it's only a movie, isn't it? But wait! This movie is called *House of Wax*, and it's the most famous 3-D movie ever. When the hideous hand first came out of the movie screen in 1953, it looked so real that audiences all over America screamed.

To understand 3-D, you have to understand first that your eyes see separately and that your brain fuses the two images together. You can prove that with your cardboard tubes. Hold just one tube up to your right eye. Hold your left hand, palm open and facing you, next to the far end of the tube. Perhaps for a second, you will see two separate images: the hole in the end of the tube, and your hand beside it. But quickly your mind will force the two pictures to merge. Then, bingo! You'll be looking at a hole in the middle of your hand!

When you look around the room, your eyes see two slightly different pictures and your brain fuses them together. The two pictures you see are flat, *not* three-dimensional. It's only when those two flat views become one that you can actually see in three dimensions. Now you might cover one eye, look around, and say, "Everything looks three-dimensional to me." But in fact, you are being guided by other visual cues: the relative size of objects, shadows, and your past experience.

In truth, the world looks flat when viewed through only one eye—or through only one camera lens. But with two lenses, mounted side by side and about 2½" apart, two pictures can be taken at once—in just the way your eyes take two "pictures" at once. That's how stereo photography was born. In the 1800s, special cameras were designed with two lenses, and special viewing devices, *stereoscopes*, were invented.

Then for many years 3-D viewing went out of fashion. And it didn't come back until the 1950s—when television was invented. You see, people stopped going to the movies because they were too busy watching the tube. So Hollywood came up with 3-D films to draw audiences out to the theater again. As with stereo photography, 3-D movies were made by shooting two versions of the same scene—by strapping two huge movie cameras together. On one camera, a filter "polarized" the light horizontally. The other camera had a vertical polarizing filter. The two versions of the film were projected simultaneously and people in the audience viewed the movie through 3-D glasses with corresponding polarizing filters. That way, the left eye was allowed to see only one version of the film, and the right eye was allowed to see the other version. Again, the brain would fuse the two pictures.

So why aren't 3-D movies all the rage today? *Eye strain.* Although 3-D viewing is exciting, it can produce headaches after a while. For that reason, you'll want to go easy on the 3-D Viewer you made.

BRINY
BEHAVIOR

BRINY BEHAVIOR

How would you like to have an animal laboratory full of sea monkeys? That's what brine shrimp are sometimes called. You can raise dozens of brine shrimp in a small jar or bowl—and then experiment with them to find out what they like, and *don't* like! The raising will take a few days, and the testing, a few minutes.

Shrimp Farming
YOU WILL NEED

2 Clean wide-mouth jars or large drinking glasses
Vial of brine-shrimp eggs (you can find these at a pet shop)
Magnifying glass
Ruler and pencil
Few tablespoons of coarse sea salt (found in grocery or health-food stores)
Measuring spoon and cup
Masking tape
1 Package dry yeast
Note: You will also need all of the things listed under "Shrimp Testing."

1 Fill 2 clean jars or large drinking glasses with tap water and let them stand, uncovered, for at least 24 hours to rid the water of any chlorine. Use this water in all of your experiments.
Do not use metal containers!

2 Take a close look at your brine-shrimp eggs under a magnifying glass. What shape are they? How many of them could sit side by side on a line 1" long? Add about one level tablespoon of sea salt to a cup of your standing water and stir until dissolved. This will make the salty water called brine. Pour the brine into a clean glass jar and mark the level of the liquid with masking tape. Bigger jars may need more cups of brine. Sprinkle a pinch of brine-shrimp eggs on the surface of the brine. Set the jar in a warm place—such as a sunny spot on the kitchen counter. You will have to check your jars every day and add more brine up to the tape mark, as needed.

3 Watch your container carefully and often during the next two days. Hold your container up to the light and use a magnifying glass to see what's happening. The new shrimp will be very tiny—almost invisible! Look for tiny white dots swimming wildly in the water.

If you don't see any new shrimp within 3 days, something has gone wrong. Start again, this time using different amounts of salt in your brine. Or try different water, such as distilled water. Or use pond water filtered through a paper towel. If you still don't hatch any shrimp, you might need a new batch of eggs—a new brand, if possible.

4 Once you see shrimp, sprinkle a few (*very few!*) grains of powdered dry yeast on the surface of the water every couple of days. If the water stays milky after a while, you are giving them too much food.

HOW MANY SHRIMP COULD YOU FIT SIDE BY SIDE?

SCHOOL RULER

PICK A SUNNY SPOT ON KITCHEN COUNTER FOR JAR

MARK THE LEVEL OF LIQUID WITH TAPE

SALT

5 Each day, spend some time studying your brine shrimp. How do they change as they grow? Females are usually larger than males. How else can you tell them apart? Watch for eggs and "babies." But don't expect your shrimp to get too big. Even the biggest "adult" shrimp are only about ½" long. In your laboratory, they may not even grow up to be *that* big.

Now that your shrimp are growing well, you can either keep them as pets (in which case you have to name *all* of them!) or you can turn your collection of brine shrimp into an animal laboratory, and put your shrimp to the test!

Shrimp Testing

YOU WILL NEED

Plastic spoon
Tall, narrow jar or glass
Construction paper or brown
    paper bag
Rubber band
Flashlight
Rectangular glass baking dish
Red and blue cellophane
Ice cube
Sandwich bag
Small cup
Red food coloring

1 Test to see how your shrimp react to light.
If the brine shrimp are already in a tall glass, great! If not, use a plastic spoon to move some of them to a clean, tall glass or bottle filled with brine. Wrap construction paper or several layers of brown paper around the outside of the glass. Hold the paper in place with a rubber band. Shine a flashlight directly down onto the surface of the brine for 3 minutes. While holding the light in place, quickly remove the paper. Where are most of the shrimp? Can you tell what direction they are swimming in?

2 Pour a jar of your shrimp-and-brine mixture into a flat glass baking dish. Stretch red cellophane over one half of the dish and blue over the other half. Watch for a while. Do the shrimp seem to prefer one end of the dish? Can you guess why?

3 See how well your brine shrimp can take the cold. Seal an ice cube inside a plastic sandwich bag and put it in the brine, at one end of the baking dish. Watch for a few minutes. How do your shrimp react? Remove the ice cube. Then repeat the experiment—but put hot water in the plastic bag instead of ice.

RED FOOD COLORING AND YEAST IN 1/2 CUP OF BRINE

ICE CUBE IN PLASTIC BAG

COVER DISH WITH RED CELLOPHANE AND BLUE CELLOPHANE

SHINE FLASHLIGHT DIRECTLY DOWN INTO GLASS

WRAP BROWN PAPER AROUND TALL GLASS FILLED WITH BRINE

RED FOOD COLORING

ST/87

4 Put some shrimp eggs in the freezer for a day or so. Will they still hatch, after they've been frozen? Put a different batch of eggs in an oven for a few hours at 150 degrees. Can you still get these to hatch when you take them out of the oven?

5 With a plastic spoon, put a few shrimp into a separate cup half full of brine. Mix a drop of red food coloring with a small pinch of yeast, and gently add the red yeast to the cup. After 5 to 10 minutes, spoon out some of the shrimp. What do you see? If the shrimp have eaten the red yeast, you should be able to see their digestive systems.

AFTERWORDS

Now that you've done so many different experiments on the brine shrimp in your animal laboratory, it's time to play that great game show — *The $15,000 Brine Shrimp Fortune Quiz!* For all the money and a trip to Salt Lake City, Utah, answer this question: Where do brine shrimp come from — the ocean, the forest, or the desert?

Believe it or not, the answer is the desert. Brine shrimp are found in America in the dry areas of the Southwest, where there is little rainfall and many lakes dry up for much of the year. When rain does fall, it fills the lakes again and also forms puddles. Brine-shrimp eggs hatch in these salty lakes and puddles, and live until the hot sun evaporates the water completely. Then the next batch of brine-shrimp eggs, which were laid while the shrimp were alive, pile up on the desert and wait for the rains to come again.

Brine shrimp are *crustaceans* — like lobsters, crayfish, and crabs. So naturally you're wondering: How did brine shrimp get out of the ocean and find their way to Utah? Actually, although brine shrimp are in the same class with lobsters, they are not really descended from shellfish and they never did live in the ocean. Instead, brine shrimp evolved from other freshwater crustaceans. They've been inland for thousands and thousands of years.

In your briny behavior experiments, you tricked your brine shrimp into thinking there was a lot of food around

when there wasn't! Brine shrimp are attracted to areas with lots of green algae, because that's what shrimp eat. Green algae absorb most of the blue light in the sun's spectrum, and that leaves mainly red light shining on the shrimp. By putting red-colored cellophane over the brine shrimp, you were able to trick them into thinking that the water was full of algae. That's a pretty good trick — much easier than having to come up with a pan full of algae!

But what happens to the eggs if the weather is very dry and hot for a very long time? When you checked out the briny behavior of your tiny shrimp, you probably found out that the eggs *will* hatch, even if they've been baked in the oven for a few hours. And they will hatch even if they've been frozen. Brine-shrimp eggs are amazingly resistant to the destructive forces in nature, because desert temperatures are often blistering at noon in summer and freezing at night in winter. Sometimes brine-shrimp eggs will sit around on the desert for

2 or 3 years before the conditions are right for them to hatch.

The Great Salt Lake in Utah is another main residence for brine shrimp, but there the life cycle is not interrupted by these long drying-out spells. Many of the brine-shrimp eggs you find in pet stores come from the Great Salt Lake. People buy these brine-shrimp eggs to raise them for food for their tropical fish, because tropical fish grow more quickly when they're fed live food.

But who eats brine shrimp in nature? Nobody. Not many other creatures live in the salty puddles and lakes. In the Great Salt Lake, there are only two kinds of flies, one species of insect, and some algae floating around — so the brine shrimp pretty much have the run of the place.

GARDEN IN A GLASS

GARDEN IN A GLASS

If you like plants and gardens, this project is for you! It is also a quick way to have a garden of your own, especially if you don't have room for one outdoors.

YOU WILL NEED

Some empty, wide-mouth glass jars with lids — the bigger the better (A pickle jar from a restaurant is great! Ask around.)

Baking soda

Some pebbles

From a gardener's shop: small quantities of horticultural charcoal, standard potting soil, vermiculite or perlite, peat moss, sharp sand (or aquarium sand), bone meal (if available), and some small plants (or find them in a vacant lot)

Pan or basin or pail for mixing soil

Old nylon stockings

Scraps of jagged rocks or pretty stones

Pieces of wood that are worn from being outdoors

Scissors, spoon

Some Plasticine or modeling clay

1 Wash and rinse your pickle jar. Sprinkle 2 or 3 tablespoons of baking soda on the inside of the lid and add some water; this helps get rid of the vinegar smell. Lay your pickle jar on its side between two magazines or books so it can't roll.

2 Wash and rinse enough pebbles to make a ½" to 1" layer on the bottom of your jar. Take ⅓ as much charcoal and wash it: Put it in a pan or basin, add water, stir, and carefully pour off the dirty water. (You might want to use a strainer.) Sprinkle charcoal evenly over the rocks. These rocks and charcoal are your garden's "drainage bed."

The charcoal acts as a filter and lets clean water run down onto the rocks.

3 Cut up some old nylons; overlap the pieces to make a thin layer to cover your drainage bed. This *separator* will keep soil from getting into the bed.

4 Mix up your soil, following this recipe: 6 cups standard potting soil, 2 cups vermiculite or perlite, 2 cups peat moss, 1 cup sharp sand or aquarium sand (if you use beach sand, be sure to wash it well — just like the charcoal), and 1 cup horticultural charcoal. If you can find bone meal, mix in ⅓ cup. If you can't get these things, try ordinary soil from your yard.

5 Now, let your imagination run wild and design your garden! You may want to make it look like a little piece of the real world with hills and pathways. Look for pretty stones or rocks and twigs. Think of a tiny plant as a tree; create a forest!

6 Use a spoon to landscape your garden. Sprinkle some of your soil over the separator. You will need enough soil to cover the roots of your tiny plants. Dig holes in the soil where you want your plants to go.

7 If your plant is potted, hold it upside down in one hand. Gently tap the rim of the pot on the edge of a table or sink. (Cover the floor underneath with newspaper, to catch any loose soil.) Slip the pot off the plant. Knock much of the dirt off the roots. Pop your plants into their holes. Switch them around until you like the way things look. Then, gently pat the soil around each plant. Take out any extra soil. Spoon a bit of water around each plant, a spoonful at a time. Don't soak the soil!

8 Screw the lid on tight and put your new *terrarium* near a bright window—but **not in direct sunlight!** (You can use plugs of Plasticine or modeling clay as wedges to keep it from rolling.) If a place is comfortable for *you* (not too hot, not too cold), it will likely be comfortable for your plants. Your plants will grow and lean toward the light, so turn your terrarium around once in a while.

9 Now, check your "sprinkler system." You should always be able to see some water droplets on the inside of the glass. If there are so many that you can't see inside the jar at all, there may be too much water in your terrarium's "atmosphere." In that case, take the lid off for a few hours. Or it may be that the sunlight is too strong; try a shadier place. If there are *no* water droplets, add some water to the soil.

Once you get a nice bit of moisture on the glass you can tighten the lid, leave it tight— and that's it! So just sit back and watch your garden grow! You'll probably never have to worry about watering your plants ever again.

VARIATIONS

■ You may want to try a terrarium with cactus plants. You will need sandy soil. Here's the formula: Mix together 1 cup potting soil, 3 cups sand, 1 cup perlite, 1 cup charcoal, and 1 cup peat moss. This garden will need very little water and very little drainage. (Cover the surface with sand to make it look like a desert.)

You can leave the lid off.

■ If you have mosses and ferns growing in your yard, you can make a sealed terrarium for these. Use the standard mix recipe but add extra peat moss. Or try planting a terrarium with whatever small plants you can find in a lawn or vacant lot.

■ Sometimes a pickle jar sitting upright with just one or two plants makes a neat terrarium. How can you decorate the lid? Make a cradle out of soft rope or cord (macrame) and hang up your garden.

LARGE PICKLE JAR FROM RESTAURANT

SMALL TWIG CAN LOOK LIKE TREE

ADD PART OF PLANT FROM POT

TOY HOUSE

DRIFTWOOD PRETTY STONE

AFTER PLANTING YOUR GARDEN, SCREW THE LID ON TIGHT

COLORED MARBLE

PAINTED EXTERIOR TO HIDE MATERIALS

PIECE OF GLASS LOOKS LIKE POND

PLASTICINE

ST/86

■ What other containers can you use for terrariums? Glasses, bowls, jars, an old aquarium are possibilities; use plastic wrap to cover them. The bottoms from the biggest plastic pop bottles are great! Just cut the bottle's top off; remove the green or black plastic bottom and plant your garden in it. Then turn the bottle bottom upside down and use it as the terrarium cover. You could make these for gifts!

AFTERWORDS

Dr. Nathaniel Ward, an English surgeon, living in the 1820s, was interested in moths. He put the cocoon of a sphinx moth in some damp soil in a glass jar and put the lid on. He looked at it often, hoping to see the adult moth getting out of its cocoon. But he also noticed that some grass and a small fern had sprouted from the soil. Being a scientist, he was of course interested in the unexpected and decided to see how long the green plants would live in the sealed jar. They were still doing fine four years later, but then the jar was damaged while he was away. (No one remembers what happened to the moth!)

How do the water drop-lets get up on the inside of the jar? You put the water into the soil. When plants are growing, their roots absorb water from the soil. This water goes up through the stem to the leaves. Inside the leaves, the plant uses some of the water to make food for itself, to grow. But there is more water in the leaves than the plant needs and this extra water is given off by the leaves. This process is called *transpiration.*

Water that has been trans-pired goes into the air in the jar in the form of a gas, or *vapor.* When this water vapor reaches the cool, inner surface of the jar, it condenses to form tiny drops of liquid water. These tiny drops run together to form the tiny droplets you can see. Gradually, these drop-lets will run down the wall and into the drainage area. From here the roots pick up the water again and the whole business repeats itself. The trip that the water takes from the soil, through the plant and the leaves, into the air, onto the wall and back into the soil is called a *water cycle.*

How can your plant breathe if the jar is sealed?

Plants take in *oxygen* and give out *carbon dioxide* — just like you do! Green plants also *photosynthesize* in sunlight. In photosynthesis, plants *take in* carbon dioxide and *give off* oxygen (and some water). So the plant recycles its own carbon dioxide and oxygen. Tiny organisms in the soil cause dead *organic* (once alive) particles also in the soil to *decompose,* or decay, gradu-ally. As they decompose, the particles release carbon diox-ide into the air in the jar.

Plants also need the element *nitrogen* to make proteins. But these protein molecules lock up nitrogen inside the growing plant. You may see your plants grow for a while and then stop. Some of the leaves may wilt, dry up, and fall off into the soil. Don't worry! Soil organisms will decay the dead leaves and release their nitrogen. This nitrogen goes back into your plants and they will perk up again. This completes the *nitrogen cycle.*

These cycles will repeat over and over again, re-creat-ing an "atmosphere" just like the Earth's. Your terrarium really is a miniature world!

TOYING WITH SCIENCE

TOYING WITH SCIENCE

These science toys are so much fun you'll want to make them as gifts to give to your friends and family...after you've made your own to play with, of course! Each should take no more than 30 minutes to put together.

SKYHOOK

Can you balance your belt on your nose? Make cereal dance around? Create a tiny ocean, complete with waves, inside a bottle? Do these sound like some great feats of magic? Guess what? They're better than magic: They're scientific!

YOU WILL NEED

1 Wooden 12" ruler
1 Uncooked egg in its shell
Some modeling clay or dough
Felt-tip markers
Yarn scraps
1 Jackknife with a heavy handle (optional; to be used by adult)
Paper, pencil, scissors
2" by 4" Piece of wood, ³⁄₁₆" to ¼" wide (basswood or plywood)
Coping saw or scroll saw

1 Try to balance a ruler across the tip of one finger. You will probably find you can only do it if your finger is at the 6" mark or right in the middle of the ruler. The midpoint of that ruler is the center of gravity — where all the weight of an object is concentrated.

2 Now try balancing a raw egg on either end, in your hand. You will find that it's too hard to do: The base of the egg is too small and the center of gravity too high. But then tap the small end, making a hole about ¾" wide across the top. Empty the eggshell and wash it out well. Place a marble-sized piece of clay or dough into the eggshell so it sticks on the center of the bottom of the shell. Now balance the egg on its larger end. In fact, you probably can't even tip it over! You've lowered the center of gravity so far down that it is impossible to topple that egg.

STICK KNIFE ABOUT 1½" FROM BOTTOM

3 Let's get back to the ruler for a few minutes. Try balancing that same ruler upright on one fingertip. Almost impossible, isn't it? That's because the center of gravity is so high, the ruler becomes very unstable. Now ask an adult to open a jackknife so the blade is at a right angle to its handle and stick the knife into the edge of the ruler at about 1½" from the bottom. That ruler will balance

THE SKYHOOK IS A GREAT GIFT!

LONG END OF SKYHOOK

BELT

on your fingertip! You have lowered the center of gravity so that it is below the ruler and in the knife and is now directly under your finger!

4 Now you're ready to make the skyhook: Trace the skyhook pattern onto thin paper and cut it out. Place the paper pattern on the wood and trace around pattern. With a coping or scroll saw, cut the wood along the line of the pattern. To use the skyhook, place a leather belt, at about the middle, into the skyhook's groove so both ends of the belt hang toward the longer part of the skyhook. Now hold the long end of the skyhook on the tip of your finger. It is amazingly stable! Place the long end of the skyhook on your nose. This "magical" toy makes a great gift!

STATIC CEREAL BOX

Have you ever walked across a carpeted room, reached for the metal door handle, and been zapped by an electrical shock that really tingled? Or have you ever rubbed a balloon on your sleeve and tried to stick it on a wall? You've been playing with electricity! This toy makes use of positive and negative electrical charges to amuse and amaze everyone.

YOU WILL NEED

Balloon
Salt, pepper
Plastic comb
Piece of nylon, fur, polyester, or wool (or wear clothes made of any of these materials)
Handful of puffed-rice or wheat cereal
1 Box with a clear plastic cover (the type that cards or stationery comes in works well)
Tape

1 If you haven't rubbed a balloon on your sleeve and stuck it to the wall, give it a try. Don't just watch what happens: Listen for the crackling sound made by the moving electric charges. If the room is dark enough, you might even see sparks.

2 Pour a little salt and pepper on a flat surface. Mix it up well. You will now be able to separate the pepper from the salt. Here's how: Rub the comb with nylon, wool, or fur (poly-

HOLD THE COMB ¾" TO 1" ABOVE AND WATCH WHAT HAPPENS?

ester works well also). Hold the comb about ¾" to 1" above the mixture and watch the pepper jump up to the comb. The salt will jump too, but not as high. You can easily remove the flakes of pepper from the salt mixture!

3 Now make the Static Cereal Box — a more permanent toy for playing with electrical charges. Put about ⅓ to ½ cup of cereal into the box. Place the clear plastic cover over it, and tape it down. Rub the box cover against you, if you are wearing something made of nylon, wool, fur, or polyester; or just rub the cover with a piece of one of these fabrics. Turn box so cover is up and watch the cereal cling to the top! If you place your finger on the cover, the cereal will dance around and shoot off the top. Have a race with someone else and see who can get one piece of cereal from one side of the cover to the other. Mark racing lines on the cover and give this toy as a present.

STORMY SEAS SODA BOTTLE

Did you ever shake up a bottle of oil-and-vinegar salad dressing and pour it over your salad — only to wind up with too much vinegar? Then you know that oil and water (or water-based vinegar) don't mix. You can pour them together, shake them vigorously, but eventually, they will go their separate ways.

YOU WILL NEED

Empty 1- or 2-liter colorless, plastic soda bottle with cap
Blue food coloring
Mineral oil (available in drugstores) or clear salad oil (you will probably need 1 pint of oil for the 1-liter bottle and 2 or 3 pints for the 2-liter bottle)
Scissors
Small scrap piece of white, bleach-bottle plastic

1 Pull off the plastic cup at the bottom of the soda bottle, if there is one, and save. Fill the bottle approximately half full of cool water. Add as many drops of food coloring as you desire to make the water a nice blue color. Mix well. Pour in the oil. If there is still space left in the bottle, add more oil or water until the bottle is filled right up to the neck.

OIL

COOL WATER AND COLORING

MINERAL OIL

2 With the scissors, cut out a tiny sailboat (or make several) from the scrap of bleach-bottle plastic. Insert the boat through the neck of the bottle. Watch what happens. It floats through the oil but stops before it gets to the blue water!

3 Close the cap very tightly. (You might want to place a small square of plastic wrap on top before replacing the cap.) Rock the bottle back and forth on its side. Watch the waves and bubbles form. To calm your seas, place the bottle back into its plastic bottom and let it set for a while. The oil and water will separate again — until your next storm at sea!

REMEMBER TO REPLACE CAP

AFTERWORDS

These science toys do indeed seem like magic tricks to anyone who doesn't understand the scientific principles behind them.

SKYHOOK

When you balance a ruler across one finger, you are demonstrating the center of gravity. In a regularly shaped object, the center of gravity is at the center of the object. An egg's center of gravity is near the center of the egg (on the inside) — yet because its base is too small, it is unable to balance itself. To balance an object, we can lower its center of gravity or widen its base.

In an irregularly shaped object, like your body, the center of gravity is any point where all of the weight of that body is concentrated — at any particular time. The center of gravity is different when we stand, sit, or bend. Anyone who skis or skates or dances knows how you must continually change your position to maintain balance: With movement, your center of gravity is constantly varying. The skyhook balances on your fingertip because the belt has pulled the concentrated weight, or center of gravity, to a point below your finger. As long as that point stays below your finger, you can balance the skyhook.

STATIC CEREAL BOX

All material things are made up of tiny particles called atoms. Every atom contains three types of particles: electrons, which are negative particles of electricity; protons, which are positive particles; and neutrons, which have no electrical charge. Electrons move about in many atoms; protons and neutrons are stationary. Generally, an object or matter has an equal number of electrons and protons, so the positive and negative charges cancel out each other. But when an object is rubbed, the electrons begin to move about and the friction created will rub electrons off one object and onto another. One object then gains more electrons, making it negatively charged.

The balloon you rubbed on your sleeve gained electrons from your sleeve's fabric and became negatively charged. As the balloon comes in contact with the neutral wall, it pushes that section of the wall's electrons away (like magnets, negative charges repel negative charges) and leaves more protons on that part of the wall, which becomes positively charged. Since opposites attract, the balloon sticks to the wall — for a while. After a bit, the negative electrons pass onto the wall from the balloon, and it falls.

Though the cereal in the box was neutral, rubbing caused the box top to become charged. That created an attraction (like the balloon and the wall) and made the cereal jump up to the cover. Touching the box top grounded the pieces of cereal and caused them to jump away, or be repelled.

STORMY SEAS SODA BOTTLE

Water has been called the universal solvent because so many other liquids and solids can be dissolved in it. Oil, however, cannot mix with water. When we shake the Stormy Seas Soda Bottle, little droplets of oil are suspended and spread through the blue water. More shaking will produce smaller droplets of oil. However, if left to sit for a while, the oil droplets cling together to re-form into one solid layer.

BLEACH
BLUES

BLEACH BLUES

Tie-bleaching is a great way to give an old shirt a new look—and it's good *clean* fun! Do it on laundry day. It will take about an hour to tie-bleach one T-shirt.

YOU WILL NEED

Glass measuring cup
Liquid chlorine bleach
Newspapers
Cotton swabs, such as Q-Tips
Construction paper in various colors
Lemon juice
Old or new 100% cotton T-shirt in a color other than white
15 or 20 Rubber bands
Washing machine
Laundry detergent
A stick for stirring

Optional:
Blue jeans
White T-shirts and a box of dye

Have you ever seen tie-dyed T-shirts? This month, you can make some fabulous patterns by using tie-dye techniques *in reverse!* Just wrap some rubber bands around an old T-shirt, throw it in the washing machine, and let the chlorine bleach do the rest of the work. While you're at it, you may want to make yourself a pair of Bleach Blues. That's what we call blue jeans that have been bleached to show all their faded glory. Find out what else you can do with bleach—and get the laundry done at the same time—with this super-cool science activity!

1 **Before you begin working with bleach:** It's a good idea to change into old clothes, just in case you accidentally splash some bleach on yourself. Bleach should be handled very carefully. Avoid contact with your skin. Don't put your hands in the bleach and don't breathe the fumes.

Hold a glass measuring cup over a sink and carefully pour in a very small amount—a few tablespoons—of liquid chlorine bleach into the cup. Then go to a well-ventilated area or do this part of the activity outside. Spread out some old newspapers to work on. Dip the end of a cotton swab or Q-Tip into the bleach and use it to draw on a piece of colored construction paper. How quickly does the bleach work? Does it work just as fast on each color of paper?

Now try squirting a little lemon juice onto a piece of construction paper. Does it bleach the paper? (Be patient. It will take longer and the results will be less dramatic. But when the lemon juice is dry, you should see a light spot.)

2 To tie-bleach one or more T-shirts, start by tying small sections of a 100% cotton T-shirt with rubberbands. Wrap the rubber bands *tightly* around each section of shirt—the tighter the better. If you want a large section to remain unbleached, then you will have to use lots of rubber bands there. *Hint:* Most rubber-band tying will make a circular pattern on your shirt. But if you want stripes, roll the shirt up like a jelly roll or sausage and then wrap the rubber bands around the sausage.

3 Fill your washing machine one-fourth full with hot water. (On most washers, you can stop the machine from filling all the way by lifting the lid.) Pour in 3 or 4 cups of bleach—about 32 ounces. Add ¼ cup of laundry detergent. Put your rubber-banded T-shirt into the washer and let it sit. (Don't close the lid because you don't want the washer to fill up any further yet!) Use a stick to stir the shirt around in the bleach. After 5 or 10 minutes, lift the shirt out with the stick and look at it. Has it faded some? If not, add more bleach to the water and let the shirt soak for another 10 minutes. Stir with the stick from time to time.

Note: When wet, your shirt won't look as faded or bleached as it probably is. Don't expect it to turn a pale, pale color. It will get lighter as it dries.

Leave the shirt in the bleach-water until it is noticeably lighter, then close the washing-machine lid and let it run through its cycle. That way the bleach will be completely rinsed from the T-shirt. Leave the rubber bands on until the shirt is completely washed and rinsed. Then take them off and either let the shirt dry on a hanger or throw it in the dryer.

HINTS FOR SUCCESS

■ Don't try to tie-bleach many different colored T-shirts together at the same time.

■ Tie the rubber bands very tightly, so that the bleach can't get to the tied parts of the shirt.

■ Use a lot of bleach. You may need to use as much bleach as water, so don't let the washing machine fill too much.

VARIATIONS

■ Try tie-bleaching a T-shirt using lemon juice—and the sun! Wrap the shirt with rubber bands, soak it in a sink partially filled with bottled lemon juice, and then put the shirt outside to dry in the sun for several hours. Don't remove the rubber bands until you think the sun has done its job.

■ If you want to make Bleach Blues—super-faded blue jeans—follow the instruc-

tions above beginning with Step 3. You can bleach blue jeans in the same washer load with your tie-bleach T-shirt *if* the T-shirt is also a dark color, like the jeans.

■ You can also tie-bleach shirts that have been dyed or tie-dyed first. Use 100% white cotton T-shirts and packaged dye. Follow the instructions on the package of dye. Make sure the dyed shirts are completely dry before you start to tie-bleach them. This is a good way to make several tie-bleached shirts to be given as gifts.

AFTERWORDS

Bleaching is a process that is performed on many products in this country, not just fabrics. Wheat, sugar, wood pulp and paper, furs, and human hair are all bleached using one of several different chemical compounds. These compounds, called *oxidizing agents*, include chlorine bleach, hydrogen peroxide, and sodium hypochlorite. All are acids, and basically they all work the same way: A chemical change takes place when the bleach reacts with oxygen. And any time a chemical change occurs in a substance, the chances are great—about 20 to 1—that the new substance will be white or colorless.

Can you see why lemon juice, an acid, might be able to bleach a cotton T-shirt if it's left out in the sun (exposed to oxygen) long enough? Actually, the sun does a very good job of bleaching fabrics, even without the help of lemon juice. You might find some examples of sun-bleaching in your house. Look at your couch or chair covers, and then find a place on the couch that *isn't* usually exposed to the sun. Furniture, wallpaper, photographs, books, papers, and even the clothing you wear are all affected by the sun's strong rays. It just takes the sun longer to bleach these things without the help of an oxdizing agent such as an acid.

Three hundred years ago, when linen and cotton fabrics were first bleached, the "acid" used was sour milk. The cloth was soaked for several weeks in sour milk, then washed and spread out on the grass for several more weeks, to bleach in the sun. Then that whole process was repeated five or six times! It took months to make cloth white.

Today, when fabric manufacturers bleach cotton industrially, the process not only whitens but also removes waxes, fats, and bits of brown husk that are present in the cotton plant. The cotton is bleached with hydrogen peroxide and other chemicals, and the cloth can be made white in a matter of *minutes!* Most cotton, linen, and silk fabrics are bleached *before* they are dyed.

The flour you eat in breads and cakes was actually bleached with some form of chlorine. You know that liquid chlorine laundry bleach is very harmful if swallowed. The secret to bleaching flour is that chlorine dioxide gas is used. In fact, the element chlorine itself is a gas. The slightly yellow or tan pigments in the flour are quickly bleached when they come into contact with the gas, but the flour itself absorbs very little chlorine.

What else gets bleached on a regular basis? Your hair does, if you swim in a chlorinated outdoor swimming pool. People often say that their hair gets sun-bleached in the summer sun, but they're only half right. It's usually the combination of chlorine from a pool and the exposure to the air that does the best "bleach job."

Wood pulp too is chemically bleached so that plain white paper can be made from trees that were obviously not white to start with. Even for wood pulp that is only going to be made into something brown—like a cardboard carton—some bleaching is required. In that case, the bleach doesn't necessarily make the pulp white, but it does remove the part of the pulp that isn't useful in paper-making.

GOOD
LOOKER

GOOD LOOKER

With a periscope, you can peek around corners without being seen! It will take less than an hour to make and decorate one Good Looker.

YOU WILL NEED

Empty box from aluminum foil, plastic wrap, or waxed paper
Masking tape
Utility knife or paring knife
2 Small mirrors about 2" × 3" (available at Woolworth's and other variety stores)
White glue (Elmer's Glue-All or similar brand)
Colored paper, paints, markers

Everyone knows what you see when you look into a mirror. You see yourself. But what happens when you look into two mirrors? If they're set up right, you can see over and around things that are blocking your view. That's how tanks and submarines get a good look at the world outside and above them. They use mirrors, mounted inside a long tube. Whether you call that tube a periscope or a Good Looker, it's a great toy and a lot of fun to use!

1 Cover the sharp, serrated edge of an empty aluminum foil or plastic wrap box with one or two layers of masking tape. This will keep you from cutting yourself on the edge while you work.

2 Use a utility knife or sharp paring knife to cut a window in the front side of the box, at one end of it. The window should be about 1½" inches long, and almost as wide as the box. *Be careful with the knife.* This might be a good time for parents to show children how to use one. Cut another window of the same size in the *back side* of the box, at the *opposite* end.

3 Put one of the mirrors on its edge in the box, so that it faces the first window at about a 45-degree angle. One end of the mirror should be wedged into the corner nearest the window. The other end of the mirror should be taped to the back

side of the box. Don't worry if the angle isn't *exactly* 45 degrees, because the size of the box will determine what angle you use. Place the other mirror parallel to the first one in a similar position at the other end of the box. (See the diagram.)

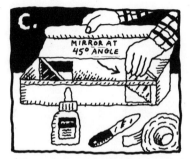

4 Tape the mirrors in place and close the box. Look through one window to see if your periscope is working. If it is, open the box and glue the mirrors permanently in place by running a thin line of white glue along each edge of each mirror. If the periscope isn't working, adjust the position of the mirrors. *Make sure the*

mirrors are parallel and that they are facing into the middle — not the corners — of the box.

D.

5 When the glue has dried and you're sure the mirrors won't move, close the lid of the box again and glue or tape it shut.

6 Decorate the outside of your Good Looker, using colored paper, wrapping paper, stickers, markers, crayons, magazine cut outs, fabric scraps, or anything else you have on hand. If you're making this periscope as a gift for someone you know, why not put her name on it as part of the decoration?

E.

■ What can you see with your Good Looker? Does it give you a good way to look at birds? What happens when you try to walk toward something you see in your periscope? What if you stick it out the window and try to look at the sky?

■ Perhaps an older person could use your periscope to see what's on top of the refrigerator…or on a shelf that's too high to reach… or to find out what's under the couch without bending over. Think of as many ways to use your periscope as you can!

VARIATIONS

Don't look now, but there are more things you can do with mirrors:

■ Set a small mirror at an angle in a shallow pan of water. Place the pan near a window so that a direct beam of sunlight hits the mirror. It will make rainbows on the wall.

MIRROR

■ To see yourself as others see you, hold two mirrors at right angles so that they form a corner or an L. Tape the mirrors together and set them on a table. Look into the corner,

where the two mirrors come together. Do you notice anything different about yourself? This is how you really look to other people. No matter how many times you've looked in a mirror, you've never seen the face that other people see —because the mirror image you usually see is backward.

Scratch your right ear, while looking into the L-shaped mirrors. Did your right ear seem to be on the wrong side? That's because you're actually looking at a mirror image of a mirror image! Try to point to a particular tooth…or your biggest freckle…or try to wipe a crumb from your face. It's not so easy! This double image is just one of the many deceptions of mirrors.

AFTERWORDS

Mirror, mirror on the wall — and in telescopes and cameras, in supermarket checkouts, in photocopying machines. In fact, just about everywhere you look you'll find mirrors being used in countless and surprising ways.

And which one is the fairest of them all? That's hard to say, but the *biggest* of them all is the mirror in the world's largest telescope on Mount Semirodriki in the U.S.S.R. It is 236.2 inches across — just 36.2 inches bigger than the Hale telescope on Mount Palomar in California. With instruments such as these, astronomers can see farther into space than they ever could before. Imagine sitting in the observer's cage in the middle of a gigantic steel tube, with your *back* to the sky. You're facing an astronomical mirror, as the light from the stars travels past you down the tube, and is reflected back to a spot just in front of you called the *prime focus.* Many people think that the lenses are responsible for the magnification provided by these enormous telescopes. But actually, except for the small eyepiece that pinpoints the prime focus, there are no lenses in these powerful reflecting telescopes. Instead, a single concave mirror gathers light from the stars and magnifies it *thousands* of times!

Unlike the concave mirrors used in telescopes, which are expensive and difficult to make, flat mirrors are fairly inexpensive and they are being used in industry in a variety of new, problem-solving ways. Mirrors are at work in the newest supermarkets and large drugstores. For several years now, laser-beam checkout systems have been used to read the Universal Product Code (UPC) prices — those vertical black lines you find on almost everything you buy. The checkout clerk passes the UPC markings over a laser scanner, and the product name and price are automatically rung up on the cash register.

But however mirrors are used, the principles of reflected light are all primarily the same. What happens with a flat mirror is this: Rays of light coming from an object in front of the mirror strike the mirror and bounce off at an angle that is equal to the original angle of light. For instance, let's say that you are in front of a small mirror at point A, and your friend is at point B. (See the illustration.) The light coming from you strikes the mirror at point C. If you drew an imaginary line perpendicular to the mirror at point C, then you could measure this angle, which is called the *incident angle.* Your friend can see you, because the light bounces *off* the mirror from C to B at an angle that is equal to the incident angle.

The interesting thing about these principles of reflected light is that when we look at reflections coming from a mirror, the light is *actually* coming from point C on the mirror. But the image appears to come from a point *behind* the mirror — point Z in the diagram. You can prove this with a camera that adjusts for distances. Stand 3 feet away from the mirror and set the camera focus for 3 feet. The picture you take will be blurry. Only if you focus the camera on the image of yourself *behind the mirror,* which is 6 feet away from where you are standing, will the picture be clear and sharp.

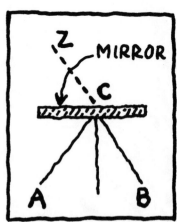

SLIME TIME

SLIME TIME

Jeepers creepers—it's slime time! Time to get down in the dirt and find out what it's like to live in the world of earthworms. It will take about an hour to build a home for worms—and then you really ought to keep an eye on them all month.

KEEP THE WORM WORLD OUTSIDE IN A GARAGE OR PATIO

COVER TOP WITH ALUMINUM FOIL

ST/88

YOU WILL NEED

Small, heavy cardboard carton
Utility knife or scissors
Acrylic "box"-style picture frame about 11" by 14", or sheet of acrylic 11" by 14"
Ruler
Pencil
Masking tape or stapler
Plastic garbage bag
Duct tape
Trowel or small shovel
Potting soil
Aluminum foil
Old bath towel

1 To make a Worm World for earthworms, you will need to construct a vertical box that is open at the top and covered on one side with acrylic. Begin by cutting your carton down to size: Cut the top part off so that you are left with a box that is 4" deep. If the bottom of the box happens to be exactly the same size as your picture frame, great! Go on to Step 3. If not, you will need to cut the box down some more.

2 Measure your acrylic sheet or plastic box-style picture frame. (Be sure to use the inside dimensions of the frame.) Now draw dotted lines on the bottom of the box to match the dimensions of the picture frame, measuring from 1 corner of the box. Cut along the dotted lines, as shown in the illustration. You will have three pieces of the box when you are done. Part A is the main part of the Worm World. Part B will form the other side of the Worm World box. Part C can be thrown away. By fitting A and B together and letting them overlap, you will have reconstructed a box, that will be 11" by 14" and open on one end. Tape or staple A and B together to make the box stronger. When you are done, you should have a box that is open on top and open at one end.

3 Now you will need to make the box waterproof. Line the bottom and sides with a plastic garbage bag, and tape the bag in place using duct tape. Don't open the garbage bag up; use it as a double layer. Be sure the box is completely covered with plastic on all of its inside surfaces. Use plenty of tape to seal the plastic to the box.

4 Place the acrylic picture frame over the box, to make the window through which you can view the worms. The picture frame should fit snugly. One end of the box will still be partly open, but that's all right. That is the top opening for your Worm World. Use duct tape to tape the acrylic to the box on three sides. Seal it well. If you are using a sheet of acrylic instead of a picture frame, use a double layer of tape to make the box stronger.

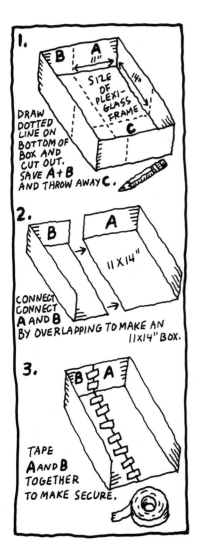

1. **B A** 11" SIZE OF PLEXI- GLASS FRAME 14" **C** DRAW DOTTED LINE ON BOTTOM OF BOX AND CUT OUT. SAVE A+B AND THROW AWAY **C**.

2. **B A** 11 X 14" CONNECT CONNECT A AND B BY OVERLAPPING TO MAKE AN 11X14" BOX.

3. **B A** TAPE A AND B TOGETHER TO MAKE SECURE.

LINE INSIDE OF BOX WITH GARBAGE BAGS AND TAPE IN PLACE. TOP IS OPEN DUCT TAPE

5 Stand the Worm World box on end, with the opening up. The box is now ready to be filled with layers of dirt. Each layer should be about 2" deep. Use alternate layers of topsoil, potting soil, and sand. Or dig some soil from two different areas— one where the soil is rich and black, another where the soil is light brown. Pack the soil down firmly as you fill the Worm World so that there are no big air spaces. To keep the earthworms from getting out, don't fill the Worm World to the top. Leave about 3 inches from the top layer of dirt to the top of the box. Water the soil so that it is quite moist but not soaking, and keep it wet by sprinkling it every few days.

6 Now it's Slime Time! Use a trowel or small shovel to dig for earthworms in your yard or in a park. (Be sure to get permission if you are digging in a public area.) Be careful not to cut the worms in half or injure them while you are digging. Handle them carefully. Place 2 or 3 good-size worms on top of the soil in your Worm World. Add a few rotting leaves on top, which the worms will eat. If you have room, you may want to keep the Worm World outside in a garage or patio. If you want to keep it indoors, cover the top with a piece of aluminum foil, punctured with small air holes. Cover the whole thing with an old towel to keep the Worm World dark.

When you are all done with the experiment at the end of the month, let the worms go—back to their real worm world!

HOW TO WATCH WORMS

■ Earthworms are night crawlers. They move around when it's dark. By putting a towel over the Worm World, you have created artificial darkness. When you take the cover off, the worms may crawl away from the light. To watch them for a long period of time, go outside at night and use a flashlight covered with a red balloon. The red light will not disturb the worms. You can go looking for earthworms this way in your yard or park at night too.

WHAT TO LOOK FOR

■ Look for the tunnels earthworms make through the layers of soil. How long will it take the worms to mix up the different layers of soil?

■ Try to see the worms as they eat. They will pull a rotting leaf partway into their tunnels and nibble on it. Sometimes they poke their heads up aboveground and eat leaves. Where are their tails?

■ Can you tell which end is the worm's head? Can you find its mouth? Are some worms fat and some skinny? Look closely: Does the same worm always stay the same shape?

AFTERWORDS

Next time you sit down to eat a BLT or a peanut butter and jelly sandwich, just remember this: You should thank your lucky worms for all the food you have to eat. Without earthworms, we would not have the kind of soil that we have on much of the earth. Without earthworms, very little food would grow. Earthworms are called "nature's plows" because as they tunnel through the earth, they mix up the soil layers, allowing air to get in and making space for plant roots to grow. They eat leaves and decaying animal fragments, which pass through them and then come out as *castings*. The castings fertilize the soil, providing food for plants. Without worms, the earth would be too hard, compacted, and lifeless to grow tomatoes or peanuts for your favorite lunch.

When you went digging for earthworms, could you tell in advance whether you would find worms just by looking at the topsoil? Was the soil a rich, black color, loose and crumbly? If so, you probably found lots of earthworms there. If the soil was hard and dry, on the other hand, with very little growing in it, you probably didn't find any. In some rich farmland areas, you could find 1 million worms on every acre of land! These earthworms can turn and churn 40 tons of topsoil per acre in a year.

Some people think that if you cut an earthworm in half, it will grow back, or *regenerate*, the missing parts. Actually, earthworms can regenerate their heads or their tails, but only if they are severed before the first 10 segments or after the last four. They can even regenerate their brains!

Did you notice a wide, lightcolored band around the body of the worms in your Worm World? That is called the saddle, or *clitellum*. Earthworms are hermaphrodites, which means that they are not male or female but *both*. All earthworms can produce eggs and can fertilize each other, but they cannot fertilize themselves. To mate, any two earthworms join together at the clitellum, fertilize each other's eggs, and then each one makes an egg case, which is deposited in the soil. If your earthworms did not have a clitellum, they were not adult worms. Maybe you had Teenage Slime Time instead!

You probably noticed that even without a cover on your Worm World, the earthworms do not try to escape. That's because they don't really want to be anywhere but inside the earth. Even when they're feeding, worms will often leave their tails anchored underground for self-protection. That way, if a robin tries to pull the earthworm out of its burrow, the worm can put up a fight. Usually, though, the robin will win the tug-of-war. Other burrowing animals such as moles will dig them out of the soil and eat them. Skunks and owls eat earthworms, too. If it weren't for these enemies, earthworms could live to be 10 years old.

Even though they have no ears or eyes, earthworms seem to have many senses. They respond to light by moving away from it, and they respond to vibrations, too. In some parts of the country, where earthworms are used as fishing bait, people use vibrations to drive worms out of the ground! They hammer a wooden stake into the ground and then beat on it. The vibrations are transferred through the soil and the worms sense danger.

SOLAR COOKER

SOLAR COOKER

If it's so hot outside you're *roasting,* stop! Don't let the sun roast *you.* Let it roast hot dogs and marshmallows instead! It will take about 45 minutes to cook up your own sun-powered ovens.

YOU WILL NEED

Empty mixing bowl
Aluminum foil
Flexible piece of cardboard about 8" by 14"
Piece of string 3 feet long
Scissors
Empty round oatmeal box, with lid
Marshmallows
3 long forks or long, pointed sticks
Hot dog

Did you know that on a clear day the summer sunshine is actually hot enough to cook meat outdoors? It's true. And the yukky truth: When you sit in the sun trying to get a tan, you're really cooking your own skin!

No one wants a roasted kid for lunch, so wear sunscreen when you're outside for long periods on a bright summer's day. (And don't be fooled by cloudy weather: The sun's rays can still penetrate and leave you with a bad burn.) Instead, let the sun go to work cooking a really delicious lunch — hot dogs and marshmallows prepared in your very own solar cooker!

1 You can make three different solar cookers and then have a marshmallow-roasting race to see which one works fastest. For the first solar cooker, all you need to do is line the inside of a large mixing bowl with aluminum foil, shiny-side up. (You may want to try two or three different bowls to see which one works best.)

2 For the second solar cooker, you need a piece of cardboard thin enough to bend. (The backing from a legal pad works well.) Cover one side of the cardboard with aluminum foil — again, shiny-side up. Then bend the cardboard into a semi-circle, with the foil on the inside of the curve. Use string to tie the cardboard in this position, as shown. This is easier to do if you wrap the string around twice and tie the knot in back.

3 Solar cooker No. 3 is really a hot-dog cooker, but you can also use it in the Great Marshmallow Toasting Race. To make the cooker, cut a long window in the side of an empty cylindrical oatmeal box. Line the inside of the box with aluminum foil. (Don't forget to put the shiny side up!)

4 Now it's cook-out time! But before you go outside, remember these rules: **Never look directly into the sun!** And be careful with the concentrated spots of sunlight your solar cooker will gather. Concentrated sunlight can burn your skin. **Also, don't look directly at any glaring or bright spot on your solar cooker.**

Outside, set your three solar cookers in a bright, sunny spot. Try to aim them so that the sun is falling directly on the foil. Then put one marshmallow on the end of each long stick or fork — and the race is on! The trick to toasting the marshmallows is to find out where the reflected sun's rays are crisscrossing. For each cooker, this hot spot will be in a different place.

Hold your hand over the bowl, and bring it down

slowly into the bowl until you find the hot spot. **But don't leave your hand there for more than a few seconds!**

For the bent cardboard cooker, you will probably find the hot spot somewhere near the center of the string — or just inside the string, closer to the foil.

The hot-dog cooker is designed to hold a hot dog on a stick *inside* the oatmeal box. So put your marshmallow on a stick and hold it in the center of the box.

Which cooker won the race? Can you figure out why one cooker works better than another?

AFTERWORDS

The sun gives out a fantastic amount of energy each day. If you could gather up all the fuel on Earth — all the gas, oil, and coal — and burn it fast enough to give off as much heat as we get from the sun, all of the fuel would be used up in three days.

Fortunately, we are not about to use up all of the fuel on Earth in three days. But Americans do use about 2,000 times as much energy today as the Colonists used in 1776. This is partly because the

population has grown quite a bit since then, and partly because we continue to require more and more energy. We use about 25% of our energy to run cars and another 25% at home, for heating and electricity. Industry uses about 20% in manufacturing steel, automobiles, and other consumer goods. And that still leaves 30% — and guess where that goes? Into *making* energy! After all, it takes fuel to do things like mine coal, drill for oil, and transport raw materials to the refineries.

Strange as it may seem, all of the fuels on Earth come from the sun in one way or another. Here's how it works: Plants use the sun's energy to make their own food. Animals and people eat the plants. When plants, animals, and people die, the decaying process eventually — after millions of years — produces what we call fossil fuels: coal, gas, and oil. They were formed from pressure and heat on dead plant and animal remains. Indirectly, the sun has provided all of the energy we use.

But now that we are using so much more energy, some experts estimate that all of our gas, oil, and coal will be gone within 500 years. That's why people are turning to solar energy as an important alternative. Several different ways were developed to harness the sun's power and put it to work on Earth. Your solar cooker demonstrated one method: *concentrating* the sun's rays into a smaller area. This is a great technique for cooking, but to heat a large area like a house or swimming pool, it's more efficient to *collect* the sun's energy and store it until you need it. Maybe you've seen houses with solar panels on the roof. First the sun warms the panels up. Then the hot panels warm up some pipes just underneath the panels. Liquid in the pipes flows down into the house and warms a tank of water. A fan blows the warmth from the water into the air ducts to heat the house.

The biggest problem with solar collectors, like the roof panels, is that the sun has to be shining for them to work. On Earth, the sun isn't always visible. But out in space, the

sun is always burning bright! Scientists have imagined that a solar power station could be constructed in space, using miles and miles of solar cells. When light strikes a solar cell, it starts an electrical current flowing. In the solar-power space station, the electricity would be converted to microwaves, and then sent to Earth. On Earth, the microwaves could be changed back into an electrical current and sent to you through ordinary power lines.

So until the sun burns out — in about 20 billion years — you'll have enough power around to at least toast a marshmallow!

SUPER
STRAWS

SUPER STRAWS

Faster than a speeding bullet, more powerful than a locomotive, able to leap tall buildings in a single bound. It's a bird, it's a plane, it's Superstraw! *Superstraw?* Yes, that device that allows you to slurp soda can be used to defy gravity and support a thousand times its weight! It should take about 30 minutes to build these super straw structures.

YOU WILL NEED

1 Box of soda straws (*not* the flexible type)
A few large paper clips
1 Pound of 1" nails or marbles, or any objects of uniform size that can be counted
Roll of plastic or masking tape
6 Or more cardboard cups, or empty soup cans
1 Tube of hobby glue
Scissors
1 Box of straight pins
1 Raw potato
2 Scraps of wood (½" to ¾" thick) the same size as the sole of your foot

Gravity is pulling us downward all the time. But we're not alone. Gravity pulls *everything* on the Earth downward toward its center. Even air, although it is invisible, has weight and is a real substance, like a solid or a liquid, and is acted upon by the forces of gravity. As a matter of fact, there is about 15 pounds of air pressure on each square inch of surface at sea level! So why don't buildings collapse and bridges fall into the waters below them? Because we've learned how to deal with gravity. We know how to use the opposing forces that exert a push against gravity.

By using straws and a few other items, you can see how the forces of gravity work—in the miniature bridges you will build and then in the great spans of real bridges on which you ride or walk. Also, see how the lowly straw can disperse pressure and can hold up a weight many times its own.

Imagine one of the first,

most primitive bridges man ever encountered. It was probably a log fallen across a stream and over which one or two people could walk at a time. Today's bridges span great rivers and bays, often for many miles. These bridges hold tons of vehicles and passengers at one time, efficiently and safely. Yet, the basic principle is the same: The upward supporting forces must be greater than the downward pull of gravity.

1 Let's make a 1-log type of bridge by using 1 straw and see how much of a load it can carry. First, make supports by stacking up two piles of

HOW MANY NAILS DOES IT TAKE TO BEND THE STRAW?

books so the height of each pile is equal to the other. (You can also use two chairs placed almost together or two table surfaces.)

Slip the straw through the loop of the paper clip. Place the ends of the straw between two piles of books. Attach a paper cup to the clip (tape it, if necessary) and begin putting nails into it or wrap tape around soup can twice (near top rim) and then slip the paper clip through, for a hanger. How many nails does it take to bend the straw? How many to make the straw collapse? Use extra paper clips and cups, if needed.

Move the two book piles, first closer together and then farther apart, and again see how many nails it takes to collapse the straw in each of those positions. What difference does the distance between supports make in how much load the straw can carry?

2 Tape another soda straw to the first one with the paper clip. You've made a *beam*. Suspend this between the two book piles. Again, hang the paper clip and paper cup from the beam. Add nails to the cup.

How many nails does it take to make the beam collapse? Does the double straw or beam construction carry more or less than twice the load of a single straw?

3 Build a beam with three straws this way: Place one straw *on top* of the other two so that

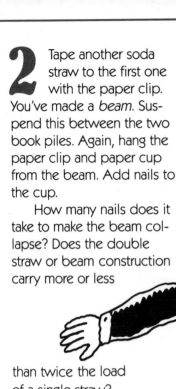

when viewed from one end, a triangle is formed. Tape them together.

Suspend the paper clip

TAPE 3 STRAWS FOR A TRIANGULAR BEAM

and cup and determine how much of a load this will carry.

Build another triangular beam, but this time *glue* the three straws together as well as taping them. Let dry and again determine how strong this one is. This is called a *laminated beam*.

4 Make your own Great Bridge: Place the two piles of books 1 straw-length PLUS another ½ straw-length apart. Use straws, tape, glue, scissors and even straight pins to make a strong bridge that will span the

distance between the two book piles. You might want to connect soda straws by sliding one inside the other. Remember also the strength in the triangular beam.

What is the greatest load it can carry before collapsing? Use the nails and cups and/or the metal food cans to find out.

5 Build a small, strong bridge with as few straws, glue, and tape as necessary, but one that can still support a heavy book. Place the two piles of books 1½ straw-lengths apart. Which bridge formation supported the book's weight?

6 Have you ever tried to push a straw through a raw potato? It is almost impossible, isn't it? But if you take that same straw and hold one index finger over one end of the straw and jab the potato with one swift stab of the other end of the straw, it will sink right into the potato. Surprised? It worked because, by holding your finger over the end of the straw, you trapped the air inside and the pressure was concentrated in the straw.

With all that pressure on one point, the straw took on a stronger force. Now let's use this same pressure idea, but let's spread it around.

Would you believe that a single straw can support your body's weight? Try this: Use sharp scissors to cut a straw into small pieces, each about ¼" long. Make each piece the same length. Glue these pieces upright on a piece of wood about as big as the sole of your shoe. Try to space them equal distances apart and let the glue harden. Lay another piece of wood about the same size over the tops of the straw pieces. Put one foot on top of the upper board and gently shift all of your weight onto the board. Have someone look between the boards. Do the straws collapse? How much weight can the straw pieces support if you put them closer together? Get more pieces to do this. How much weight can the straw pieces support if you make them longer? Shorter?

AFTERWORDS

Just as your skeletal system (along with your muscular system, of course) holds you up, the skeletal system of a structure such as a bridge keeps IT up. Any bridge or structure you see has two kinds of forces acting upon it. One force, *gravity*, is pulling down toward the center of the Earth. The *skeletal* or structural system of the bridge is counteracting that force, exerting an upward force to keep it from collapsing. In your first experiment, the straws supported between the book piles were being pushed "up" by the surfaces of the books, while the cup of nails was trying to pull the straw bridge down toward Earth.

Did you notice that the straw was not absolutely rigid? Part of the downward force helped change the shape of the straw: It sagged at the middle with the weight of the cup full of nails. Just how much it bends at the middle depends partly upon how far the middle of the straw is from its supports. The farther the middle was from the book-pile supports, the greater the bend (or distortion) of the straw.

Two straws side by side should have been able to carry twice as much load.

But a beam made of *three* straws, and especially when glued together tightly, made a much stronger structure. A triangle was created in which the load carried by any one straw was more easily shared with the other two. In building construction, a beam that is made up of a number of smaller pieces fastened together is called a *laminated beam*. Laminated beams can hold more than the sum of each of their individual parts.

Surprised that one straw, cut into small pieces and placed on end, could easily carry your body weight? If you sat in a bucket hung from one soda straw stretched between two tables, it wouldn't hold you! This is because of *pressure* —the force pushing down on a surface.

You can spread a large downward force over a small area, especially if you have many small areas. If you step on one nail sticking up out of a board, it could go right through your foot. The force of your body weight is concentrated on the tiny area at the point of the nail—terrific pressure! Have you ever seen someone lying on a bed of nails? The many nails are close together so that no one nail is given enough pressure to puncture the skin. But be careful getting up and lying down!

The skeleton of a skyscraper has several vertical columns of steel. These columns carry all of the weight of the building and act just like the small pieces of straw that were glued upright. Because they carry the load vertically, there is very little distortion of the columns.

When you built the Great Bridge, you might have used a number of triangles. Triangles can share loads more easily than squares or rectangles. The triangular parts of a bridge have the same advantages in carrying a load as did your three straws fastened together. The famous American architect Buckminster Fuller pioneered the use of triangles in buildings. He called his design a *geodesic* (earth-shaped) dome. Your public library would have a picture of one. Perhaps you could try building one with straws. Imagine how it would be to live in such a house!

KITCHEN BOTANY

KITCHEN BOTANY

Kitchen Botany is a good activity to begin about an hour before dinner. After you are finished, eat the less sweet produce with a dip. Eat the sweet produce with fondue for dessert. Recipes are included.

YOU WILL NEED

At least one of the following from each group:
Cucumber, zucchini, watermelon
Apple, pear, quince
Tomato, grape, blueberry
Plum, cherry, peach
Carrot, celery, parsnip
Onion, garlic, shallot
Cabbage, cauliflower, broccoli
Cutting board
Knife
Magnifying glass (optional)
Ingredients for Dip and Fondue (optional)

Have you ever eaten a flower? What plant parts do you eat? A tomato is a vegetable—isn't it? This activity deals with fruit and vegetables you eat all the time. They will help you answer these questions. You'll take a look and then take a taste. And then you can grow your own garden with what's left over.

1 Put all of the produce on a table. Place all fruits in one pile and all vegetables in another. How did you decide which pile to put each piece in? Was your choice based on color or taste? Was it based on the section in which each can be found in a grocery? None of these things will help you separate the fruits from the vegetables. The following will.

2 Place a cutting board and knife on the table. Being careful with the knife (or ask an adult to help), cut each piece of produce in half crosswise.

3 Examine each half carefully. Use a magnifying glass if you have one. If you find seeds or pits inside, the piece of produce is a fruit. If there are no seeds, it is a vegetable. Reclassify, or regroup, your produce into separate piles of fruits and vegetables.

4 Eat the vegetables with a dip as an appetizer before dinner, or put them in the refrigerator for later use in cooking.

5 Line up the fruit on the table. Fruits come in all shapes and sizes. They can be mushy or crunchy, with seeds or with a pit. There are names that describe these

differences. Try to match each piece of fruit with its descriptive name.
- Pepo (PEEP-o): a fleshy fruit with many seeds inside and a harder rind outside.
- Pome (like ROME): a fruit with a hard covering around its seeds.
- Berry: a pulpy fruit that has many seeds.
- Drupe (DROOP): a fruit with a hard pit that covers one seed.

6 Refrigerate the fruits, or eat them for dessert with honey or cream or chocolate fondue. Save some seeds to grow your own houseplants.

FONDUE

Melt one package of chocolate chips in a double boiler. Ask an adult to show you how. Dip the fruit in it with forks.

If chocolate is something you avoid, serve the fruit with several kinds of cheese.

DIP

Mix one package of dried onion soup mix with one 16-ounce container of cultured sour cream. Chill before serving.

VARIATIONS

Some fruit seeds and vegetable parts can be used to grow beautiful plants.

■ Plant orange or other citrus seeds in potting soil and water them. Keep them in a warm place until seedlings develop, then move them to a sunny spot.

■ Apple, peach, pear, and plum seeds need a cold period before they will grow. Scratch the seeds with sandpaper and plant them in plant moss and keep them in the refrigerator for about two months. Then plant them in potting soil and watch them grow.

■ Make hanging planters from root vegetables such as carrots, beets, turnips, etc. Cut off the top two inches of the vegetable. Scoop out the core. Hang the plant upside down by putting toothpicks into the vegetable and hanging it with a string. Keep the scooped-out hole filled with water. You may have to fill it several times each day. Green leaves will grow out from the vegetable top, up and around your "planter."

AFTERWORDS

When you divided your produce into fruits and vegetables, you were *classifying* it. Classification is the act of sorting objects by certain rules, or criteria. When you sorted your produce, the criterion was that all produce with seeds is fruit. Classification is an important scientific tool. People who study plants know that plants with similar flowers, fruits, leaves, or growth forms are often related. Just like people, these related forms are grouped into families.

The squash family includes cucumbers, pumpkins, watermelons, cantaloupes, and gourds; it also includes summer squashes such as zucchini and winter squashes such as acorn. These fruits grow on vines with five-sided stems that creep along the ground or climb by wrapping their small tendrils around other plants, fences, etc. They have fairly large leaves, often shaped like maple leaves. We generally eat only the fleshy parts of the squash family fruits, but cucumber and zucchini are eaten flesh, seeds, rind and all. There are even recipes for fried squash blossoms and squash blossom soup in some cookbooks.

The tomato family is sometimes called the nightshade family. Some nightshades, like the deadly nightshade of Europe, are extremely poisonous. Its more tasty family members include tomatoes, potatoes, peppers, and eggplant. Appropriately, tobacco also comes from this family. Members of this family usually have flowers with five petals and fruit in either a pod or berry with many seeds.

The rose family includes apples, cherries, strawberries, pears, plums, almonds, and peaches. Members of the rose family can be as small as a rosebush or as large as a tree. Their flowers commonly have five rounded petals. Rose hips, high in vitamin C and often used in herbal teas, are the fruit of a rose flower much like the ones seen in gardens. In ancient times, the rose was used medically. It was a favorite of the Romans, who spread its culture wherever their armies conquered.

Vegetables are also classified into families. Members of the mustard family include broccoli, cauliflower, cabbage, radishes, turnips, brussels sprouts, kale, horseradish, and mustard plants. Members of the mustard family are sometimes called crucifers (KROOS-i-ferz), from their Latin name, which describes the crossshape of the four petals of the mustard flower. The mustard that we spread on sandwiches is made from ground mustard seeds mixed with vinegar or oil and spices. While most mustard plants are fairly small, the black mustard plant of Palestine can grow up to 12 feet tall and have birds singing in its branches. Even a phenomenon like that does not defy classification.

ALIENS

ALIENS

Is there life in outer space? Will alien beings ever come to Earth? Scientists have several methods of finding out and here's one way. It will only take you 30 minutes to set up the experiment, but you may not see results for several weeks.

YOU WILL NEED

4 Empty jars with lids
Hot water
Measuring cup
Saucepan
Unflavored gelatin
Spoon
Pen or marker
Paper
Tape
Scissors
String

Extraterrestrials…alien life-forms…little green kids from outer space. Are they out there—and, if so, what do they look like? What if the aliens aren't *large* visible beings that walk and talk? What if they are too small to be easily seen?

That is the problem scientists had to deal with in the 1960s and '70s, when the Viking spacecraft was being designed to land on Mars. Scientists needed a way to detect *any* life-forms—even tiny, microscopic ones, like bacteria. One of the experiments designed for the Viking project was called Gulliver. In the Gulliver test, "sticky" string would be dragged across the surface of Mars. Then the string would be put in a container with "food," so that if any life-forms were stuck to the string, they would be nourished and grow.

You can try a version of the Gulliver experiment yourself here on Earth. Who knows? Maybe you'll find life-forms in places you never even *suspected* could sustain life—maybe in your closet or under your bed!

1 First, you will need to sterilize your jars, to remove any life-forms (germs, for instance) that are already there. To do this, wash the jars and then pour boiling water into them. The jars will be hot, so **don't touch them now.** Let them stand until they are cool. Sterilize the jar lids in the same way, by pouring boiling water on them. **Be very careful when using the stove to boil water.** You may want to have an adult help you with this.

2 Measure 2 cups of very hot tap water into a saucepan. Add one packet of unflavored gelatin and stir until the gelatin is completely dissolved. You may need to heat the water and gelatin over low heat to help the gelatin dissolve. Pour ¼ cup of gelatin into one of the jars and screw the lid on tight. Label the jar "control." Then pour ¼ cup of gelatin into each of the other three jars.

3 Cut 3 pieces of string, each about 15 inches long. Dip one of the pieces into the remaining gelatin in the pan and leave it there for a minute, until the string is soaked. Then take the string and drag it across the floor somewhere—under your bed, across the living-room rug, across the basement floor, or wherever you like. Put the string into one of the jars and screw the lid on. Label the jar with "Rug" or "Basement" or wherever the sample came from. Soak the other 2 pieces of string in gelatin and go outside to repeat the experiment. You might want to drag one of the strings across the grass or dirt and the other across the sidewalk. Label these samples, after putting each into a jar, and put the lids on both of them.

4 Now, wait and watch. Check your jars for life-forms every day. It might take two weeks or more before you see a change in the gelatin—or on the string. And remember: The life-forms you are looking for are tiny, like bacteria. They probably won't grow into big, ugly green blobs! But the important

VERY IMPORTANT! WAIT FOR JARS TO COOL...

REMINDER! BOIL WATER WITH ADULT PRESENT

CONTROL JAR

DRAG STRING ON FLOOR, UNDER BED, BASEMENT OR ANYWHERE YOU LIKE. GO OUTSIDE ON GRASS AND DIRT.

thing is that you're discovering life-forms where you didn't think they existed!

Is there anything happening in the control jar? If so, that shows you that your jars had bacteria in them even before you put the string samples in.

VARIATIONS

■ Leave the sticky string outside for several hours before sealing it in the jar.
■ Punch holes in the lids of the jars so that any alien beings present will have an air supply.

■ Use a string soaked in apple juice and a string soaked in gelatin to collect life-forms outside. Leave them both in the sun for an hour or so. Does the apple juice attract a life-form different than the kind attracted to the gelatin?

WHAT IS A CONTROL?

Whenever you conduct a scientific experiment, you are asking a "what if" question. For instance, you might ask "What will happen if I pile 726 cement blocks on my bicycle?" The answer is that the bike would be crushed! If you actually tried this experiment, you wouldn't need a "control," because you would have no doubt that the results came from only one cause: the cement blocks!

But for some experiments, you can't be sure what is causing the results. For instance, this month you are asking "What will happen if I drag some string on the ground and then seal it in a jar with gelatin?" If something starts to grow in the jar, are you sure it came from the string? Or did some life-forms fall into the jar while you were dragging the string around? In these cases, you need to set up two sam-

ples. You do your experiment on one of the samples, and leave the other sample—the control—alone. If the results you were looking for occur only on the experimental sample and not on the control, then you know exactly what caused the results.

AFTERWORDS

Searching for life on Mars or any other planet is a lot more difficult than you might think. For one thing, scientists must make sure that they don't contaminate the planet they are visiting by bringing along life-forms from Earth. When the Viking mission was launched in 1975, both of the space-crafts—Viking 1 and Viking 2 —had to be entirely sterilized to kill all bacteria or other microorganisms that might be present. Can you imagine pouring boiling water on a spaceship? Actually, the Vikings were heated to 235 °F, then sealed inside a shield to keep out microorganisms.

Landing on Mars wasn't easy. On Earth, parachutes are often used when we want to drop people or objects out of the sky and land them safely on the ground. But the atmosphere on Earth is very dense compared with the atmos-

phere on Mars. That means that when parachutes open above Earth, the atmosphere is "thick" enough to push against the parachute material and cause it to slow down. On Mars, the atmosphere is so thin that it doesn't create much resistance. To jump out of a plane above Mars, you'd need a very big parachute!

To solve this problem and help the Viking lander get from the orbiter to the surface of Mars, scientists decided to use a combination of parachute and rocket engines. The rockets would help the lander set itself down gently. Unfortunately, the rockets themselves posed a new problem, because they tended to blow the soil in every direction. Scientists wanted to be sure the lander didn't mess up the soil directly surrounding the landing area, because that was the soil that would be sampled for the biology tests. Eventually, a better design for the rocket engines was found.

Did scientists find evidence of life on Mars? The results were mixed. Biologists generally agree that life-forms can be detected three ways: (1) You could look for evidence that some kind of food had been produced; (2) you

could look for evidence that food had been consumed; and (3) you could look for changes in the atmospheric gases—which is another way of saying that someone, or something, is breathing. (On Earth, atmospheric gases change when plants give off oxygen or when people exhale carbon dioxide.)

Although scientists didn't find any signs of food being produced, they did discover, during several experiments, that atmospheric gases changed quite a bit. However, the changes were not necessarily the kind that would indicate the presence of life-forms. Other experiments showed results that could easily have been caused by the presence of microorganisms—or could have been caused by strange chemical reactions on the planet. And when the Martian soil was finally analyzed, no organic molecules were found.

So what's next? Another trip to Mars—or maybe to that great, gassy planet Jupiter? Someday, you may be on board when another sticky string is cast into the vast universe, in search of aliens.

LAWN PAPER

LAWN PAPER

The amount of time it takes to make Lawn Paper depends upon the drying method you choose. The paper itself can be prepared in about two hours.

YOU WILL NEED

Grass clippings
(about one handful)
Scissors, measuring cup, paper towel
Blender or food processor
Water, newspaper
Piece of window screen
(about 5″ × 8″)
Dishpan or tub or sink
Iron (optional)

Here's something to do with grass clippings that you probably never thought of: Make paper! Even though most of the world's paper is made from wood, many plant materials can be used: cotton, celery…even grass clippings. So grab a handful, and try it!

1 Use the scissors carefully to cut the grass into pieces about ¼″ to ½″ long. You will need about one cup of chopped grass. Put the grass into the blender.

■ Cut a paper towel into ¼″ pieces. Put the pieces in the blender with the grass.

PRESSING

LETTER

PICTURE FRAME

DECORATIONS

MOM DAD AND ME

CARDS

SHAPES

■ Add three cups of water to the paper and grass in the blender.

2 Blend the grass-paper-water mixture (called slurry) for three to five minutes or until it feels soft and smooth. Keep a close watch on your blender. If the grass is too long or there isn't enough water, your blender may have to work too hard and it will overheat. Add extra water so the grass doesn't get caught in the blades.

3 Pour off the excess water from the slurry and throw it away.
■ Put the screen into the dishpan or sink.
■ *Slowly* pour the slurry onto the screen in a thin, even layer. Use your hands to gently pat down, smooth any lumps,

and fill in any holes. Flatten the slurry on the screen so it's smooth and flatter than a pancake.

4 Lay newspaper on top of the slurry. Pick a piece that doesn't have much dark print or else the wet lawn paper may absorb some of the dark ink.
■ With one hand under the screen and the other hand over the newspaper, carefully turn over the screen, slurry, and newspaper.

5 Press down hard on the screen to squeeze out water. Slowly peel up the screen so that your paper is left on the newspaper. If the paper sticks to the screen, keep pressing more water out of it.

■ Now keep pressing your lawn paper with dry newspaper. Press as hard as you can for a few minutes to flatten the grass and bind the fibers into paper.

6 To dry your paper, you can:
■ put it outside in a sunny spot.
■ put it in a solar greenhouse to dry it faster.
■ iron it dry in 10 minutes. Put the iron on the *cotton* setting. Protect your paper from heat by sandwiching it between layers of paper towels or newspaper.

7 When it is dry, carefully peel it away from the newspaper. Use your lawn paper for a special purpose:

■ Write a letter to a special person.
■ Take a picture of your family on the lawn or in your park. Frame the picture on a piece of lawn paper.
■ Have a lawn party with lawn-paper invitations and decorations.

VARIATIONS

■ Try making paper with dried grass instead of fresh, or cut up the leaves of a tree or shrub. How is this paper different from paper made from fresh grass?
■ Make colored paper by adding food coloring to the slurry. Or try using the newspaper comic pages in Step 4. They will also add color.
■ Be fancy. Press a dandelion or other pretty weed into the wet paper before pressing and drying.

■ Be creative. Shape the slurry on your screen into a shape, such as a dragon or a flower. Find things on your lawn to use as eyes and other details. Then press and dry it.

AFTERWORDS

Paper is a surprisingly recent invention. It was created less than 2,000 years ago by the Chinese. Conquering Arabs discovered this Chinese paper in 704 A.D., but it wasn't until about 600 years ago that paper came into common use in the West. In the Middle Ages, reading and learning were encouraged. This increased the demand for paper. As the demand increased through the centuries, the quality of paper was improved by experimenting with different raw materials.

Today, paper is made from cellulose pulp, which is found in all plant tissues and fibers. Fibers are thick-walled plant cells that support plant tissue. They are hollow tubes about ⅛" long and thinner than a hair. These tubes are reorganized to form thin sheets when paper is made. These thin, long cells give paper its toughness and flexibility.

Although any fiber may be used to make paper, certain fibers make higher quality paper than others. Linen is an excellent material for paper because its fibers have notches that help them stick to each other. Grass and straw have short, smooth fibers that cannot make strong papers alone. Adding other fibers, such as those in paper towels and newspaper, to grass fibers makes the lawn paper stronger. That is because paper towel and newspaper fibers are less smooth than grass fibers and help in binding the reorganized fibers into paper.

Today, about 95% of the world's paper is made from wood pulp, and there are about 12,000 types of paper manufactured. We use paper products every day. An average family discards one ton of paper each year—the amount of paper produced from 17 trees. That is a small forest every few years! Because of this, recycling centers have become valuable coordinators for the re-use of waste paper. Not only does recycling save trees, but it also uses 30% to 40% less energy than producing paper from new wood pulp. Try recycling a piece of your own lawn paper to prove this point.

Grass is almost everywhere—so why isn't grass made into paper? Grass is grown in wide-spread areas and the crop is bulky. Transportation costs alone make large-scale grass paper production more expensive than wood-pulp paper production. Also, the grass supply and its price vary from year to year. So grass paper production is held back by the difficulties of grass supply, rather than by any technical difficulties. These difficulties don't have to stop *you*. As long as you have a nearby lawn, park, or grassy traffic island, you can produce your own lawn paper.

SERIOUS LOAFING

SERIOUS LOAFING

Rise and shine! It's time to find out what makes bread rise. You'll need at least 4 hours to get from mixing to baking to eating. In the meantime, mmm-mmm—what a wonderful smell!

YOU WILL NEED

2 Large drinking glasses
2 Packages active dry yeast
1 Tablespoon sugar
All ingredients for Good White Bread, as listed in recipe
Large and small bowls
Measuring cups
Small saucepan
Wooden spoon (or hand-held or electric mixer)
Kitchen utensils
Plastic wrap
9" by 5" by 3" Loaf pan
Pot holders or oven mitts

EXPERIMENTING WITH YEAST

What does yeast actually do and how does it make bread rise? To find out, try this easy experiment. In a large drinking glass, mix 1 package of active dry yeast and ½ cup of *very* warm water (100° to 115°F.). Label this YEAST. Stir well to dissolve the yeast. In another glass, mix 1 package active dry yeast, ½ cup very warm water, *and* 1 tablespoon sugar. Stir well. Label this YEAST AND SUGAR. Set both glasses in a warm spot and watch what happens. Within 10 or 15 minutes, you will know which yeast mixture is producing a gas called *carbon dioxide*. That gas is what makes bread rise. Keep this experiment for several hours and watch to see how long the yeast keeps on working, making carbon dioxide bubbles. What happens when the yeast runs out of gas?

MAKING BREAD

1 Make sure that you have permission to use your stove and oven. You may need an adult's help. Take the middle rack out of the oven. Preheat oven to 400° (375° if you are using a glass baking pan) and assemble all the ingredients for the Good White Bread recipe.

INGREDIENTS FOR GOOD WHITE BREAD

1 Package active dry yeast*
½ Cup very warm water (100° to 115°F.)
2 Tablespoons sugar
4 Tablespoons (½ stick) melted butter
1½ Cups warm milk
1 Tablespoon salt
5 to 6 Cups unbleached or bread flour
*For an even fluffier loaf, try 2 packages of yeast.

In a small bowl, combine the 1 package active dry yeast and ½ cup very warm water. The water should be 100° to 115°—it will feel quite warm but not burning hot to your fingers. Stir well. When the yeast is mostly dissolved, add 2 tablespoons sugar. "Proof" the yeast by letting the mixture sit for 5 to 10 minutes. It will start to bubble and foam like your yeast-and-sugar experiment. If it doesn't foam up, either the water is too hot or the yeast isn't fresh.

2 While the yeast is proofing, melt 4 tablespoons butter and add it to 1½ cups warm milk. Stir in 1 tablespoon salt. Now you will begin adding flour. All together, you will probably need 5 or 6 cups flour, or more. Start by adding 3 cups flour to the milk-and-butter mixture, and stir with a wooden spoon, or with a hand-held or electric mixer. Then add the yeast mixture to the dough and mix well for 1 minute. Add 2 more cups of flour, or enough to make the dough pull away from the sides of the bowl. You may need to add all of the flour. The dough should not be too sticky because in the next step you are going to knead it.

3 Turn the dough out of the bowl onto a floured board or floured countertop and knead it until it is smooth and elastic—for about 5 to

10 minutes. To knead the dough, push into the dough with your fist or with the heel of your hand. Then fold the sides of the dough over and repeat the process. Turn the dough frequently as you knead it. Keep adding flour to the board and to the dough if the dough gets too sticky. When the dough is smooth and elastic, divide it into two equal pieces. Put half the dough in a clean, buttered bowl. Turn it over once or twice to coat it with butter. Cover dough with plastic wrap and let it rise in a warm place until it is double in bulk—twice its original size. This may take from 1 to 2 hours. Check it frequently.

4 In the meantime, butter the inside of a 9" by 5" by 3" loaf pan. Put the other half of the dough into the loaf pan and brush the top with water. Bake it immediately—*without letting it rise*—on the lowest rack in a 400° oven (375° if your loaf pan is glass). Bake for 40 minutes and then check it by carefully knocking on the bread. (Use pot holders to pull the pan from the oven.) If the bread sounds hollow, it's probably done. You should also carefully turn the loaf out of the pan and knock on the bottom, to make sure it sounds hollow too. Allow the bread to cool on a rack, and then slice it and try it. Even though it hasn't risen much, you can still eat it. How does it taste?

5 Wash the loaf pan and butter the insides again. Now check on the dough in the bowl. When it has doubled in bulk, punch it down. How long did it take for the bread to

rise? Is it more or less time than it took for your yeast-and-sugar experiment to fill the glass with foam? Turn the dough out of the bowl and knead it again for 3 or 4 minutes. Shape it into a loaf and put it in the buttered pan. Cover with plastic wrap. *Allow it to rise a second time, until it is double in bulk.* Brush the top with water. Bake it on the lower rack in a 400° oven (375° for glass pans) for 40 to 45 minutes. Knock on the loaf, as in Step 4, to see if it's done.

Most bakers say that bread should cool completely before you slice it. But who can resist hot, freshly baked bread? How does it taste, compared with the first loaf of bread that was not allowed to rise?

AFTERWORDS

Yeast is a microscopic plant that can change sugar into carbon dioxide and alcohol. This process is called *fermentation.* In your first experiment, the yeast converted the sugar-water to carbon dioxide, and you saw the glass fill up with foam. The foam is actually many tiny bubbles of carbon dioxide gas. Carbon dioxide is the colorless and odorless gas we exhale when we breathe.

The rising of bread is simply like blowing up a million tiny balloons scattered throughout the dough—except that *you* don't blow up the balloons. The yeast does. To make bread rise, you must give the yeast some sugar, and you must distribute the yeast throughout the bread dough by kneading it. Otherwise the bread will rise in some places and not in others. Did you find a few large holes in your loaf of bread? If so, you probably didn't knead it enough. Holes in a loaf of bread mean that larger patches of yeast were gathered there, giving off a whole lot of carbon dioxide.

But why does yeast give off carbon dioxide in the first place? Because yeast is a living plant and it behaves like all living cells. It uses oxygen to maintain life. When you take in oxygen and give off carbon dioxide, the process is called *respiration.* Even dandelions use oxygen from the environment and then give off carbon dioxide as waste material. So why can't we use dandelions to make bread?

The answer is that most plants, including dandelions, use up the carbon dioxide they produce in a process called *photosynthesis*—the making of food for the plant. Dandelions make their own sugar—they don't need a glass of sugar-water to help them grow. And the carbon dioxide produced by the dandelion is used right away by the dandelion itself. Yeasts, on the other hand, are not green plants and do not make their own food. They feed on other plants and animals. So the carbon dioxide they produce is not needed for photosynthesis. It is not used up and it can be seen as bubbles in the glass. It can also be used to make bread rise.

Another byproduct of yeast's respiration is alcohol. Alcohol is produced quickly and in large amounts when yeast is combined with sugar in a *low-oxygen* environment. When wine and beer are made, the yeast is not *aerated*—not allowed to get much oxygen—and consequently more alcohol is produced. Very little alcohol was produced by the yeasts in your bread recipe, because so much air was present when you were mixing and kneading the dough. Any alcohol produced was burned off during baking.

Yeast is what makes beer alcoholic, and the carbon dioxide from the yeast gives the beer its carbonated or fizzy taste. Some bread recipes even call for a can of beer, instead of yeast, to make the dough rise! Again, the alcohol in the beer burns off when the bread is baked.

Yeasts are in the air and often settle on foods that are left uncovered or unrefrigerated. Then the yeasts go to work converting the sugars in the food into carbon dioxide and alcohol. If you've ever left a jug of apple cider, tightly closed, in the refrigerator for too long, it probably became alcoholic-tasting. Yeast strikes again!

YUMMY YOGURT

YUMMY YOGURT

What's white and sour and comes with fruit on the bottom? A grouchy polar bear who's been tramping around in a cherry orchard! Or maybe the answer is yogurt—which you can make yourself. In that case, it's not quite so sour and it comes with fruit on the top! Allow about 45 minutes to make a yogurt warming box, and one hour more to prepare the yogurt itself. It will take 7 to 8 hours for the yogurt to "cure."

YOU WILL NEED
Small cardboard box, or
    insulated food cooler
6-Inch stack of newspapers
6 Plastic trash bags
1 Quart fresh whole milk
Saucepan
Candy thermometer
4 8-ounce cups or jars
Measuring spoons
Small bowl
2 Teaspoons fresh plain
    yogurt (check expiration
    dates for freshness)
Aluminum foil
Masking tape, pen or marker

What's the difference between yogurt and milk? Just one thing: bacteria. Yogurt is made with bacteria that grow and multiply and cause the milk to "set" into a custardy, creamy, delicious food. You can make your own yogurt for less than half the price of commercial yogurt—and all you need is a little culture to get you started!

1 To make yogurt, you will first need to make an insulated "warming box" to keep the bacteria happy. Start with a small cardboard box from the grocery store, or use an insulated food cooler. Line the bottom and the four sides of the box each with a stack of newspapers at least 1" thick. You may want to enclose each stack of newspapers in a clean plastic garbage bag, to keep everything dry and clean. Make a sixth pack of newspapers 1" thick, wrapped in a plastic bag, to use as a lid. If you are using a food cooler, add some newspapers anyway, as extra insulation. Try to leave just enough space inside the warming box for the number of cups or jars you plan to use.

2 Place the insulated box in a spot where it can remain undisturbed for the next 8 hours. Have the clean cups or jars ready nearby. Heat 1 quart of fresh milk (don't use old or sour milk) slowly in a large saucepan until it reaches 180°F on the candy thermometer. Pour the milk into the cups or jars, and set them close together in the warming box. Do not fill the jars all the way to the top—leave about an inch of room at the top. Place the candy thermometer in one of the jars and check it every few minutes. When the milk in the jars has cooled to 110°F, it's time to add the yogurt starter. It may take 30 to 45 minutes for the milk to cool to this point.

3 Now you must work quickly. Take 1 tablespoon of milk from each pint of milk you are using. If you started with 1 quart of milk, you will need to take a total of 2 tablespoons of milk from the jars.

It's okay to take 1 tablespoon from each of two jars, and forget about the other two jars for the moment. Put the 2 tablespoons of warm milk—110°F in a small bowl and add 2 teaspoons of fresh plain yogurt. This is called adding the "culture." Don't use any more than 1 teaspoon of yogurt for each tablespoon of warm milk. Stir it up gently. Now divide this mixture evenly among *all four jars* of warm milk in the insulated box. Gently stir, to mix the yogurt culture in well. Cover the jars if you have lids. Place a sheet of aluminum foil on top of the jars, as an extra cover. Put the top layer of newspaper insulation on as a lid.

4 Leave the jars in the warming box undisturbed for 6 to 8 hours. Then check the yogurt. If it has set, put it in the refrigerator to cool. If the yogurt does not set within 8 hours, see the Trouble Spots list.

TROUBLE SPOTS

- Was the plain yogurt starter too old—past its expiration date?
- Was the milk too hot—warmer than 110°F—when you added the starter?
- Did you jiggle or open the warming box too much during the eight hours?

VARIATIONS

- Find out what happens to the bacteria in your yogurt starter by adding it while the milk is still hot—hotter than 110°F. You can set up a controlled experiment with four cups of milk. With masking tape and a pen, label one cup "Plain—no starter." Don't add any starter to this jar. Label the other three jars with the temperature that the milk was when you added the starter. Try adding ½ teaspoon plain yogurt starter to 8 ounces of hot milk while it is still 180°F. In another jar, add the ½ teaspoon of starter when the milk is 150°F. In the fourth jar, add the starter when the milk is almost cool enough, say about 115 to 120°F. Let all four jars sit in the insulated box. Begin checking the samples after four hours. Did the yogurt made with hotter milk set more quickly? How does it taste compared to the yogurt made with cooler milk?

■ Try adding a little more starter yogurt—1 or 2 teaspoons per cup of milk—to see how it affects the taste.

■ Add 1 or 2 tablespoons of powdered milk to make a thicker, firmer yogurt.

JAM TIME
If you like your yogurt with sweetened fruit, try adding a few tablespoons of strawberry jam or peach preserves to the homemade yogurt. Mix well and enjoy!

AFTERWORDS
Making yogurt might seem like magic to someone who doesn't understand bacteria. After all, you simply heat up some milk, add a tiny bit of yogurt and—poof!—you've got *more* yogurt! It would be great if you could do that with chocolate.

But yogurt has a secret ingredient: bacteria. When the right kind of bacteria are introduced to a container of warm milk, they begin to "feed" on the *lactose,* or milk sugar. They use the lactose as a source of energy, and change it into lactic acid. That's why yogurt is sour, while milk is almost sweet. As the milk becomes sour, the protein in the milk begins to break down and it *coagulates,* or sets. That's what makes the milk become firm, like a custard.

Usually two different kinds of bacteria are found in yogurt: *Lactobacillus bulgaricus* and *Streptococcus thermophilus.* These two bacteria really work well together; they stimulate each other's growth. But they don't both grow at the same time. *S. thermophilus* grows better at lower temperatures, while *L. bulgaricus* grows better at higher temperatures. If you introduced the yogurt starter while the milk was still quite warm, you probably produced a more sour- or tart-tasting yogurt. That's because *L. bulgaricus* took over; it produces more acid than *S. thermophilus* does.

What happened if you introduced the bacteria to the hot milk while it was still almost 180 degrees? You probably killed the bacteria! Most bacteria will be killed at that temperature, which is why you heated it in the first place. You didn't want to be growing other, possibly harmful kinds of bacteria while you were making your yogurt.

The sourness of yogurt depends almost entirely on which kind of bacteria are allowed to take over while the yogurt is fermenting. To make a mild, creamy yogurt that isn't too tart, you need to encourage the *S. thermophilus* to grow. Of course, some of that bacteria must be present in your starter to begin with. The problem is that *S. thermophilus* doesn't live too long in the refrigerator, so if your yogurt starter isn't fresh, the bacteria probably aren't there.

Yogurt has the reputation for being a healthy food—and it is. Basically, it has the same nutritional value as the milk it was made from, but yogurt is easier to digest. The fermentation process—the process of changing milk sugar into lactic acid—helps to partially digest some of the protein in milk. Yogurt and milk are also both very high in calcium, which is necessary for your bones and teeth. But in order for your body to use calcium, it must be absorbed in an acid environment. Only about 20% to 30% of the calcium in milk can be absorbed by your body. Since yogurt is acidic on its own, the calcium in yogurt can be absorbed more easily.

Yogurt is believed to be one of the oldest foods in the world—and it is eaten by some of the oldest people in the world. People from the Balkan countries are known for eating a lot of yogurt, and many of them live to be 100 years old! Maybe the yogurt contributes to their longevity, or perhaps some other factors are responsible. Enjoy your homemade yogurt, even if you don't live to be 110!

CAMERA CREATIONS

CAMERA CREATIONS

Put together your own photography studio and see what develops! This activity should take you about 45 minutes to complete.

YOU WILL NEED

1 Empty round oatmeal box
Black spray paint or
poster paint
Sharp knife
Small piece of aluminum foil
Tape, scissors, needle
2 Pencils, 1 pen
2 Red balloons
Flashlight
Package of 5" by 7" single-weight photographic paper, #1 or #2 (see Note)
Wristwatch with a second hand

Important: *You will also need all of the darkroom supplies listed on page 91.*

Note: All photographic supplies are inexpensive and readily available at camera stores and photography shops. *Do not open the photographic paper until you reach Step 6!*

Believe it or not, you can actually make a camera by simply putting a tiny pinhole in one end of a light-tight box. That's how the earliest cameras worked! You'll be amazed at the sharp quality of the pictures taken with an empty oatmeal box.

1 Paint the inside of an empty oatmeal box with black spray paint or poster paint. Do the same to the inside of the lid.

2 Use a sharp knife to cut a circle about 1½" in diameter out of the *center* of the bottom of the box. Save the cardboard circle, because you'll need to use it later: It will be the "lens cap" for your camera.

3 Cut a square piece of aluminum foil slightly larger than the hole you made in the bottom of the box. Tape the foil to the *inside* of the box so that it covers the hole. Be sure to keep the foil smooth, and tape around all four sides of the foil

PAINT INSIDE OF BOX WITH BLACK PAINT
OATME
1½"
ALUMINUM WITH PINHOLE

square so that no light can get through. Now use a needle to make a pinhole in the aluminum foil in the *exact center* of the bottom of the box. The hole should be just a pinhole —**no larger.**

4 Fit the cardboard "lens cap" back into place and tape it so that it can be opened like a flap or door. Tape a pencil along the outside of the oatmeal box, and tape another pencil parallel to the first one, about 2" away from it.

TAPE PENCILS TO BOX
M
TAPE "LENS CAP" SO THAT IT CAN OPEN LIKE A FLAP

5 Before you can load your camera, you need to make a "safelight" — a dark-red light that won't ruin the photographic paper when turned on in a completely blackened room. To make a safelight, cut off and discard the "necks" from two red balloons. Stretch the remaining pieces of balloon across the end of a flashlight, one on top of the other, like a double pair of socks.

STRETCH BALLOON ACROSS END OF FLASHLIGHT LIKE A PAIR OF SOCKS
CUT OFF ENDS

6 Take your safelight, oatmeal-box camera, scissors, tape, and unopened pack of photographic paper into a *completely* dark closet or bathroom. It is best to do this step at night and turn out all the lights in your house, so that *no* light will leak in through the cracks around the windows and doors. Turn on your red flashlight. Remove the lid from the oatmeal box; make three tape loops (sticky-side out) and set them in the lid. Now you may open your package of photographic paper. You will see that the photographic paper is wrapped in a black paper liner or envelope, inside the cardboard package. Always keep the photo paper inside the black paper envelope and keep the black envelope inside the cardboard package. **Also remember:** *Never* turn on the room lights until the photographic paper is put back in its package.

7 Take out only one sheet of photographic paper and cut a circular piece to fit inside the oatmeal box lid. The smoother, shinier side of the paper is called the emulsion side. Put the circle of paper in the lid with the emulsion side facing up. Press it flat; the tape loops in the lid will hold it in place. Put the lid on the box tightly, and your camera is loaded!

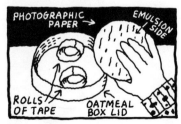

PHOTOGRAPHIC PAPER →
EMULSION SIDE
ROLLS OF TAPE
OATMEAL BOX LID

8 Go outside the next day and set your camera on something solid. The pencils along the sides of the box will keep your camera from rolling. If it's windy, you might also need to steady the box by putting one hand firmly on top. Point the camera at whatever you want to photograph, and open the lens cap. Leave the lens cap open for 1 minute if you are photographing in very bright sunlight, 2 minutes on a somewhat cloudy day, or 3 minutes if it is very overcast outside. (**Note:** You may need to experiment with the exposure times. A one-minute exposure on a bright, sunny day works best.) While the lens cap is open, you must not move the camera!

Jot down a description of the subject matter you photograph each day. Also write down the exposure times — the number of minutes and seconds you had the lens cap open. Later, when you develop the pictures, you can look at these notes to find out which exposure times worked best.

SET CAMERA ON BOX OR SOMETHING SOLID

"KEEP STILL FOR ONE MINUTE PLEASE!"

At night, go into your darkroom with the red flashlight, and remove the exposed circle of paper from the camera lid. *Put it back in the package of photographic paper.* Cut another circle and load your camera again. After you've taken 7 or 8 pictures, you will be ready to develop your pictures in the darkroom part of this activity. The instructions for all the darkroom work are printed on pages 91 and 92. Good luck!

HINTS FOR SUCCESS:

■ Take pictures of things that stand still. If you want to photograph people, they will have to remain absolutely still for 1 to 3 minutes.

■ If your pictures come out completely black, your camera might have a leak. Make sure the lid fits very tightly. Also, use shorter exposure times.

■ When loading your camera, **do not** cut out extra circles of photographic paper in advance. Otherwise you won't be able to tell which ones are exposed and which ones are unexposed.

■ You might want to make two or three cameras at once.

Then you can take more than one picture per day.

AFTERWORDS

Believe it or not, the first cameras were whole rooms completely sealed off from light, except for a tiny hole in one wall. The light coming in through the hole projected an image on the wall opposite the hole—an image of the scenery outside the room. People stood inside these *camera obscuras* (the term means "dark chamber" in Latin) and observed the giant images that seemed to appear like magic.

The camera obscura and your pinhole camera are both based on a very simple scientific principle: Light rays always travel in a straight line. When you look at a tree, you can see it because light rays strike the tree and reflect toward your eye. Of course, the light rays are also being reflected in every other direction at once, too; so no matter where you stand, you'll always be able to "catch some rays" and see the tree.

But how do the camera obscura and the pinhole camera "see"? Figure #1 illustrates that, of all the light rays being

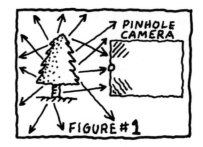

FIGURE #1

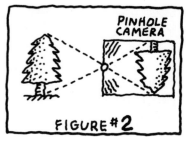

FIGURE #2

reflected, only one beam of light, the one that is entering the camera pinhole, is important. The pinhole "captures" that beam in the camera obscura and lets you view it alone—without any other beam of light striking the same space. If you were to take away the pinhole and open the front of the camera, all kinds of light rays would strike the rear wall at once, bleaching each other out, and you wouldn't be able to see an image at all.

In Figure #2, you can see why the image in the camera appears upside down. The light ray from the top of the tree strikes the *bottom* of the rear wall of the camera. And of course the light ray from the bottom of the tree strikes the *top* of the rear wall.

The camera obscura has existed since at least 1038, and it was put to many uses. In the 1200s, scientists realized that they could avoid eye damage by using a camera obscura, rather than the naked eye, to observe the sun. In the 1500s, early astronomers used the device to view eclipses, discover sunspots, and even to measure the sun, moon, and stars. And finally, in 1558, a 20-year-old Italian scientist named Giovanni Battista della Porta published a widely read book called *Natural Magic* in which he described the camera obscura. In fact, Battista della Porta was often credited, in error, with having invented the device. However, he *did* come up with a new use for it. He realized that the camera obscura could be used by artists, who could trace the image projected in the camera and thus have a completely accurate and life-like drawing of a landscape, still life, or person.

Soon after, the *portable* camera obscura was developed. At first, tents were used because they could be moved from place to place. Later, people realized that it wasn't necessary to actually stand inside the camera to see the image. A box version of the camera obscura was developed, using a ground-glass focusing screen, much like the aluminum-foil screen in your oatmeal-box camera. Through the use of a mirror placed inside the box, artists were able to focus the image on the box lid. Then they could lay their paper on top of the glass, and trace away!

DARKROOM INSTRUCTIONS FOR PINHOLE CAMERA

This activity is best done at night, when you can make your kitchen or bathroom *completely* dark.

YOU WILL NEED

1 Small package of Dektol
    paper developer
Measuring cup
Long-handled spoon
    for stirring
3 Large glass or plastic bowls,
    each with at least
    1½-quart capacity
Water
1 Teaspoon white vinegar
1 Small package of
    photographic fixative
Sink
Tongs
Photographic paper,
    wristwatch, and safelight
    from camera activity
Paper towels
5" by 7" Sheet of glass
    or Plexiglas, such as glass
    from a picture frame
Sponge for clean-up

Note: All darkroom work should be done with water and chemicals at 68°F. When you are mixing the chemicals, you can judge the water temperature by feel. At 68°F, it will feel very cool, almost cold, but not ice-cold. The water should not feel warm at all.

Caution: Photographic chemicals can stain your clothing, and are irritating to the skin. Avoid touching the developer and fixative. Wash any spills thoroughly with clear water. You might also want to protect the floor from spills by using newspapers or a plastic dropcloth.

1 Mix the Dektol developer according to the directions on the package, and pour it into a large glass bowl. Half fill another bowl with water and add 1 teaspoon of white vinegar to it. This second bowl is called the "stop bath." In a third bowl, mix the photographic fixative according to the directions on the package. Place these bowls in a kitchen

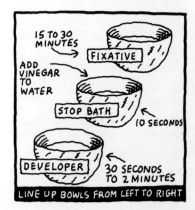

15 TO 30 MINUTES → FIXATIVE

ADD VINEGAR TO WATER →

STOP BATH ← 10 SECONDS

DEVELOPER ← 30 SECONDS TO 2 MINUTES

LINE UP BOWLS FROM LEFT TO RIGHT

or bathroom. Choose a room that can be made completely dark. The bowls should be lined up from left to right: first, developer; then, stop bath; then, fixative. Partially fill the sink with water.

2 Make the room *completely* dark except for the red safelight. Have ready your wristwatch, tongs, paper towels, and photographic paper. Open the package of paper and take out just one of the circles that have been exposed in your camera. Slip it into the bowl of developer with the emulsion side facing up, so you can see what's happening as it develops. Rock the bowl gently, every 10 seconds. Very soon you will see a picture starting to appear. Let the picture develop fully: It should take anywhere from 30 seconds to 2 minutes. Don't let the picture turn black!

3 When the picture looks right, use the tongs to remove it from the developer and drop the picture into the stop bath. After 10 seconds, lift the picture out of the stop bath and *drop* it into the fixative. Rock the fixative bowl gently every once in awhile. Let the picture sit in the fixative for 5 to 10 minutes. (It is all right to turn the room lights on after the picture has been in the fixative for 2 minutes.) Then put it in a sink of cool water for 15 to 30 minutes to rinse.

Important: *Rinse the tongs off in plain water before you develop another picture.* You must never get any of the fixative or stop bath into the developer.

4 While the first picture is fixing, you can go on to develop others. Always work from left to right…from developer, to stop bath, to fixative, to the washing sink. When all of the pictures are washed, dry them between two paper towels. You can speed up the drying by resting them over a warm light bulb or near a heater.

You will notice that your pictures look strange. Everything that should be dark is light, and vice versa. This is actually a paper negative — just like the film negatives from a regular camera. Now you can print a paper positive from this paper negative.

THIS IS A NEGATIVE…

PUT LIGHT ON FOR 15 SECONDS

SHEET OF GLASS TO HOLD THEM TIGHTLY

PAPER NEGATIVE FACE DOWN

PHOTO PAPER EMULSION SIDE UP

5 When the paper negatives are dry, go back into the darkroom. Take with you a small sheet of glass or Plexiglas. Tape the edges of the glass so that you don't cut yourself. In the darkroom, with only the red light on, put a new piece of photographic paper on the countertop or some other flat surface. The shiny, emulsion side of the paper should be facing up. Put a dry paper negative *face down* on top of the photographic paper. Put the sheet of glass on top of both, to hold them tightly together. Make sure that *all* other photo paper is closed up in its package. Now flick the room light on, then off very quickly, just once. It should be on for only about 1 second — or less. Develop, fix, wash, and dry the new piece of photographic paper just as you developed the paper nega-

tives. If your exposure was right, you will have a positive picture of the scene you photographed earlier in the week!

HINTS FOR SUCCESS

■ Never turn on the room light until you have checked to be sure that all the photographic paper is put away.

■ Keep the red flashlight at least 4 feet away from the photographic paper if possible. Even this safelight can "fog" the paper after a while. Keep the paper closed up in its package except when you are actually using it.

■ When developing pictures, you may bring the red flashlight very close to the paper for a few seconds to see how the developing is coming along.

NOTES

NOTES

NOTES

NOTES